7x7 COOKING

7x7 COOKING

The Art of Cooking in a Small Kitchen

Hope Korenstein

Photography by
Jennifer Silverberg

SKYHORSE PUBLISHING

Skyhorse Publishing books may be purchased in bulk at special discounts for sales promotion, corporate gifts, fund-raising, or educational purposes. Special editions can also be created to specifications. For details, contact the Special Sales Department, Skyhorse Publishing, 307 West 36th Street, 11th Floor, New York, NY 10018 or info@skyhorsepublishing.com.

www.skyhorsepublishing.com

10 9 8 7 6 5 4 3 2 1

Library of Congress Cataloging-in-Publication Data is available on file.

ISBN: 978-1-62087-688-6

Printed in India

The following photos were previously published in *Feast Magazine*: 4, 10, 116, 126

For my mother

Table of Contents

Introduction

More and more, it seems like cooking is treated as a source of entertainment, rather than a means of getting a delicious dinner on the table easily. Turn on the television and you're bound to see a bunch of people competing to make something delicious out of cow intestines. Or else witness a celebrity chef de-boning a duck or whipping lumps of crab meat into mousse. It might be fun to watch, but it's not something most people will try to imitate at home, especially after a long day at work. Better to call the take-out place around the corner and get delivery food for half the price of the cost of a whole duck. Or take a short trip to the supermarket prepared foods counter, which has everything from eggplant parmagiana to fried chicken and sesame noodles. No wonder people eat out an average of 4.2 meals per week!

If you live in a small city apartment, you have even less incentive to cook than the average suburbanite with a kitchen island and a six burner stove. If you're lucky, your apartment has a separate kitchen, rather than a row of miniature appliances lining one wall of the living room. With a small kitchen and dozens of quick dinner options only a phone call away, it becomes easy to avoid cooking altogether.

But there's a catch. Take-out food is, with rare exceptions, soggy and cold by the time it arrives. Prepared foods at the supermarket have probably been sitting under a heat lamp for ten hours or more. The stuff just doesn't taste good.

There is another way! You don't have to choose between eating out, microwaving a plastic container of macaroni & cheese, or eating expensive but nonetheless soggy take-out every night. In my experience, cooking can be a relaxing and satisfying experience, even if your kitchen is nothing more than a mini refrigerator, a mini stove, and a sink lined up along a wall. Certain adjustments can be made.

What does it mean to cook in a small kitchen? First of all, a small kitchen means that you don't have a whole lot of counter space. Let's say you've become obsessed with cooking a recipe that involves stuffing, glaze, and three different sauces, all of which need to be prepared separately but assembled at the same time. Cooking this recipe will require simultaneous use of lots of different bowls, saucepans, and platters—and you don't have the counter space to support all of that. Before you know it, you've got a colander full of food resting in the sink, and several pots of food balanced precariously on your couch. That is if you have enough pots, pans, and bowls to spread all over your apartment. Generally, if you have a small kitchen, you also have small cabinets, which hold only a limited amount of cookware, gadgets, and assorted kitchen tchotchkes.

And speaking of gadgets you don't have, let's talk about dishwashers because you don't have one! So after you've finally finished cooking the aforementioned recipe with stuffing, glaze, and three sauces, every single dish you own is dirty and needs to be washed—by hand. The list of appliances you don't have, by the way, is not limited to the dishwasher: you also don't have a large food processor, or a deep fat fryer, or an electric mixer. All of those recipes that sound great and look easy, but require something to be deep fried, or blended, or otherwise whizzed into mush, are not an option.

SIDE NOTE: For those lucky few who do have some spare counter or cabinet space, manufacturers have some budget friendly appliances available that can help cut down on some of the work—known as mini- or hand held appliances. (Think mini-food processors, handheld mixers, and emulsion blenders.) These won't be able to do the same work load as their larger counterparts, but they work in a pinch if you're cooking for two.

The problems of cooking in a small kitchen are multiplied during the summer. When it is hot outside, it is even hotter inside, especially in an apartment that may not have central air conditioning, or even very good ventilation. Under those circumstances, turning on the oven pretty much amounts to turning the entire apartment into a sauna.

Since the recipes in this book are geared toward how I live and cook, and also the budget I work with, it's easier for me to list all of the stuff that the recipes in this book don't have:

- Tons of ingredients—okay, that's not always true, but if I do use a lot of ingredients, it's mostly spices. Usually the ingredient list is small and manageable.

- Lots of different components to a single dish that must be separately prepared—which would take up too much space and create too many dirty dishes.
- Processed, puréed, or foods made extremely small by using something other than a sharp knife. But you will need a seriously sharp knife. Believe me, it's worth the extra money, and a good knife lasts forever.
- Deep fried foods. Unlike those chefs you see on television, I do not have a deep fat fryer sunk into my countertop.
- Grilled foods. I don't have a barbecue. I will, however, teach you to love your broiler.
- I don't use any expensive meat or fish. You won't find a dish that sounds pretty good, and then caviar, or lump crabmeat, or something incredibly expensive is added in to make the dish even more appealing.

Just to even the score, I thought I would throw in a list of ingredients that I use all the time and some techniques that show up quite a bit in my recipes:

- Lots of chicken, fish, and pasta. I use as much cheap protein as I can find. Mussels, for example: they are inexpensive, are easy to cook, and taste great. Salmon and cod are usually not very pricey, and are very versatile. Chicken, obviously, the canvas of any cook. Cheaper cuts of meat like flank steak. Pork is also inexpensive, low in fat, and you can do almost anything with it.
- Chilies. I like spicy food. You can obviously tone down the spice in my dishes, but be prepared for a little heat.
- Quick sautés, bakes, or broils. I work all day, so I don't necessarily want to spend two hours in the kitchen getting dinner together. People in the suburbs usually grill if they want something fast and tasty. My recipes demonstrate that you can cook fast, tasty food without a grill.
- Low pot and pan usage. I also tend not to use bowls or dishes where a plastic bag or the roll of aluminum foil can be used instead. (I can already feel the eco-guilt setting in.) First of all, I don't have very many pots and pans. Second of all, I hate washing dishes, so I try to keep the dish dirtying to a minimum.

- Foods that require little or no cooking. I live in a small apartment, with iffy air conditioning. When it is hot outside, I still want to eat, but the last thing I want to do is heat up the kitchen (and, by extension, the rest of the apartment). There are lots of recipes in this book that can be prepared without turning on the oven, and with a minimum amount of heat.
- Alternative suggestions. I sometimes point out alternative ingredients in my recipes, but let me say this: my recipes are suggestions only. These are the dishes that work for me, and that I cook all the time, but you should use them as a starting point, and experiment with vegetables and flavors that you like!

Have fun and eat well!

Five Tips to Cooking Great Food

Of course, there's no guarantee that everything you cook will taste great, but there are a few things you can do—especially if you haven't done much cooking – that can help you out.

1. Cook what is in season. Not only will your food taste better, but you'll also save money. When your grocer can get produce from local farmers, it costs much less than when he has to schlep it here from another country. And if it came from another country, chances are it was picked long before it's hitting your grocery cart, so it's not even very fresh.
2. Use good ingredients. This is kind of a corollary to cooking what is in season, but it's just as important. Try to use good cheeses. Believe me, freshly grated parmesan cheese is not even on the same planet as the stuff you shake out of a container. Buy some good quality olive oil for salads (but don't bother using the good olive oil for cooking).
3. Read the whole recipe before you start cooking. This may seem obvious, but I often find myself glancing at the ingredient list and then glazing out the rest of the recipe. If you read the entire recipe, and make sure you understand what you need to do, then there's no danger that you'll get halfway through the recipe and then get stuck.
4. Taste the dish as you cook it. This is so important! If you taste the food as you cook it, you can make sure that it will taste good when it hits the table. And if you taste it and it doesn't taste good to you, think about what might make it better. Which brings me to my next suggestion:
5. Use salt! One of the main reasons that a new cook's food doesn't taste good is that there isn't enough salt. If the flavors taste dull, or bland, salt can magically brighten up the dish. While I'm on the subject of salt, I should mention that I use kosher salt in all of my recipes. It is available at every grocery store. The big difference between kosher salt and table

salt is the size of the salt crystals. Kosher salt has larger crystals, which are easier to pinch and measure with your fingers. I store kosher salt in an old jelly jar, so it is easy for me to grab a pinch of salt and throw it into what I am cooking. (If I tried to grab table salt, it would slide right through my fingers.)

A FEW WORDS ABOUT SERVING SIZES: I am of the opinion that leftovers in the refrigerator are like money in the bank, so I usually cook meals with a built-in plan of leftovers. Most of my recipes serve two (in my case, me and my husband) with leftovers for lunches or another meal during the week. If you are less enamored of leftovers than I am, you can always cut recipe amounts in half.

Equipment List

While I'm not prepared to say that you absolutely, positively must possess the following equipment list, it will certainly make your life easier in the kitchen.

A GOOD QUALITY SHARP KNIFE: A sharp knife is a beautiful thing. Suddenly, it is easy to cut food, and it takes so much less time than fighting those vegetables with an old, dull knife. Of course, it also takes much less time to cut yourself so be careful!

SILICONE-TIPPED TONGS: Next to my knife, this is the tool I reach for the most when I'm cooking. I use tongs basically as an extension of my hand, for grabbing hot food, turning food over, and stirring. Make sure to buy silicone-tipped tongs, which won't scratch the pots and pans.

ONE LARGE POT: If you don't have one already, I'd like to suggest a dutch oven, rather than a pasta pot. A seven-quart dutch oven has a wider mouth than a pasta pot, which makes it easier to stir things like soups and stews. Some dutch ovens are super heavy (and expensive) but you can find cheaper, aluminum dutch ovens that are reasonably priced.

TWO PANS: A twelve-inch skillet and a ten-inch skillet should do the trick. Try to find heavy pans, because they will conduct the heat better than lighter ones and food is less likely to burn. I like non-stick skillets, but take a careful look at the pans; if it looks like the non-stick coating might come off, chances are that it will come off. And it will come off into your food, not the ideal seasoning...

A RIMMED COOKIE SHEET: This is perfect for roasting vegetables. The rim makes it easy to toss everything with your hands without the vegetables jumping overboard.

A TWO-SIDED CUTTING BOARD: Make sure you designate one side of the board for raw chicken and meat, and the other side for everything else.

A COLANDER: For draining pasta and rinsing vegetables.

A LARGE BOWL: For tossing salads and for the occasional baking project.

A BOX GRATER: For shredding cheese and grating vegetables.

A VEGETABLE PEELER: For carrots, potatoes, etc.

A ZESTER: I have to include this because I use mine all the time. It's great for grating hard cheese and taking the rind off of oranges and lemons. It is also, hands down, the best way to grate ginger.

A WOODEN SPOON: For stirring.

MEASURING CUPS: For measuring.

A POTATO MASHER: For mashing.

Salads and Starters

NO LETTUCE REQUIRED: I love greens, but a few years ago I developed an aversion to washing and drying lettuce. The result is that I created some easy salad recipes including only ingredients that are washable, dryable and chop-able. I've since overcome the aversion (it helps that I can buy pre-washed greens when I just don't feel like pulling out the salad spinner) and so there are several salads using greens included here as well.

Vinaigrette

I use this on every kind of salad you can imagine, and it always tastes great. It's also incredibly easy to make. I usually throw some together on a Sunday and then use it all week. I think it tastes much better than any of that bottled junk.

1 tsp Dijon mustard
3 Tbsp lemon juice, cider vinegar or white wine vinegar
Salt and pepper
⅔ cup good olive oil

Mix together the mustard and vinegar or lemon juice. Add a big pinch of salt and a few grinds of pepper. Slowly whisk in olive oil, or shake everything together in a glass jar with a screw-top lid. That way, you can store the vinaigrette in the same container that you made it in.

NOTE: You can add garlic, thyme, cilantro or any other herb you like.

Panzanella

Serves two

Panzanella is technically a bread salad, and you are certainly welcome to add cubes of stale bread to this recipe, but I've found that I prefer this salad with a crusty loaf of bread alongside. Add some cheese, maybe some prosciutto, and a glass of wine, and you have a great summer meal, without ever turning on the stove. Make this at the end of the summer, when the tomatoes are at their best. I don't use vinegar here—the juice from the tomatoes adds plenty of acidity.

4 large, very ripe tomatoes
1 small red onion
2 Kirby or Persian cucumbers, or ½ English cucumber
½ ball fresh mozzarella cheese
½ red pepper
Handful of basil leaves (optional)
3 Tbsp olive oil
Salt and pepper to taste
½ cup olives (I like Calamata olives)

Coarsely chop the tomatoes and throw them in a large bowl with some salt. Thinly slice the red onion and add that. Cut the cucumbers into thick rounds and add to the bowl. (Peeling is optional.) Cut the cheese into cubes and add to the bowl. Cut the red pepper into thin strips, then cut each strip into thirds and add that. Tear up the basil leaves, if you are using them, and add. Dress with olive oil and season with salt and pepper. Add the olives, toss everything together and serve.

NOTE: I usually don't pit the olives, but you have to remember to warn whoever you are feeding, unless you dislike the person and want them to break a tooth . . .

Lemon vinaigrette

This is terrific tossed with steamed broccoli or asparagus, but you can use it on whatever you like. Be sure to pour the vinaigrette on the vegetables when they are still hot; that way, they will really absorb the flavors.

1-2 cloves of garlic
½ tsp salt
Fresh ground black pepper, to taste
1½ Tbsp lemon juice
4 Tbsp olive oil

Smash the garlic with the side of your knife, sprinkle it with salt, and continue mashing with the side of your knife until it is paste. Put it in a shake jar or small bowl, add the black pepper, lemon juice and olive oil and whisk or shake together well.

Thai mango salad

Serves four, or two with leftovers

This is a very refreshing, hot weather salad. As always, the chili is to taste. This salad benefits from sitting around a while and tastes better the day after it has been made.

Juice of one lime
2 tsp honey or sugar
1 tsp grated ginger
1 Tbsp fish sauce, or soy sauce, or even just a big pinch of salt
½ tsp Sriracha or any hot sauce you like

2 small cucumbers, like Kirby or Persian
1 small red onion
1 mango
½ small jicama
3 scallions
Bunch of mint
Bunch of cilantro

In the bottom of a bowl large enough to hold the salad, squeeze in the lime juice, and let the honey or sugar dissolve into it. Add the ginger, fish sauce and Sriracha, and stir together. Taste and correct for seasoning. If the dressing is too spicy, some more honey will cut the heat.

Cut the cucumber, red onion, mango and jicama into medium dice. Slice the scallions and chop the mint and cilantro. Dump everything into the bowl, and stir until the vegetables are coated.

ON JICAMA: Jicama is a crunchy root that has some sweetness and a little starchiness; it has been described as a cross between an apple and a potato. It is terrific in salads or served alongside dips. You can certainly leave it out here, but I think it adds a nice crunch.

DIP

Roasted red pepper-feta dip

Serves 8-10 as a starter

This dip is a terrific starter that is off the beaten path of the standard, mayonnaise-based dip, and it's incredibly easy to make. You will need to whiz everything together, but if you don't have a food processor, those mini choppers sell for very little money, don't take up much space, and are seriously handy. Or, you could finely chop everything, for a chunkier dip. I serve this with vegetables and pita chips. The horseradish gives the whole thing just the right kick. I love roasted peppers, and they are a cinch to make, but if you don't have the time or inclination, you can certainly substitute a store-bought jar.

3 red bell peppers
⅓ cup feta cheese
3 Tbsp olive oil
Juice of 1 lemon
1 clove garlic, chopped
1 Tbsp prepared horseradish

First, roast the peppers. Simply stick the whole peppers under the broiler and cook, turning, until they are black on all sides, which will take about 5 minutes per side. Put the cooked peppers in a paper bag to cool.

When the peppers are cooled, peel and seed them. Blend them with the rest of the ingredients. Taste the dip—it might need a touch of salt.

ON ROASTED PEPPERS: They are so easy to make and are terrific on sandwiches, in salads, or even tossed with some pasta and your favorite cheese. Rinse off the pepper and place it whole under the broiler. Broil until it is charred all over. (You'll have to rotate the pepper to get uniform blackness.) Remove the pepper and put it in a paper bag, to steam off the skin. When the pepper is cool, the skin should slide off the flesh, and it should be very easy to pull out the stem and seeds and to pull the pepper into strips. Place them in a jelly jar or plastic container with a pinch of salt and a splash of olive oil. They will keep for a week.

Middle Eastern chopped salad

I got the idea for this salad from a restaurant in my neighborhood. The secret to the salad is the oregano. Of course, you can dice the vegetables as finely or coarsely as you want.

6 Tbsp olive oil
Juice of one lemon
Salt and pepper to taste
½ tsp dried oregano or 1 Tbsp fresh oregano

1 red pepper, diced
1 small red onion, diced
2 Persian or Kirby cucumbers, diced
2 plum tomatoes, diced
Handful of radishes, diced
⅓ cup of feta cheese, diced
1 can of chick peas, drained

In the bottom of the bowl in which you intend to serve the salad, whisk together the olive oil, lemon, salt, pepper and oregano. Toss with all of the vegetables and serve.

Gravlax

Serves 10–12 as an appetizer

This recipe is such a show-stopper, and it is so ludicrously easy to make that I had to include it. The only thing you need is time—about two days, to allow the salmon to cure. Seriously, the hardest part of this dish is slicing the salmon after it has finished curing. This is delicious served with small rye or pumpernickel rounds.

- ⅓ cup kosher salt
- ⅓ cup sugar
- 1 Tbsp ground black pepper
- 2 pounds of salmon fillets, center cut
- 1 large bunch dill sprigs

Mustard Sauce

- 2 Tbsp white wine vinegar
- 1 Tbsp sugar
- 4 Tbsp Dijon mustard
- ⅓ cup olive oil
- 2 Tbsp chopped dill

Mix together the salt, sugar and pepper. Cut the salmon in half lengthwise. Dry the flesh with paper towels, then sprinkle it evenly with the salt-sugar mixture and rub it in slightly. Place the dill on top of one half of the salmon, then place the other salmon half, flesh side down, on top of the dill, so that you have a sort of sandwich of salmon, with the skin sides out and the dill in the middle. Put it in a dish, cover it with foil, and weigh it down with cans or bricks or whatever you have around. Put it in the refrigerator for 36 hours, flipping it every 12 hours.

Meanwhile, make the mustard dill sauce by combining all the ingredients.

When the salmon is cured, remove the dill and as much of the salt-sugar mixture as possible. Thinly slice the salmon against the grain and serve.

My mom's broccoli salad

Serves four

My mom has been making this salad for as long as I can remember, and she always receives rave reviews. This is great in the summer and can easily be doubled or tripled for a crowd.

1 head broccoli
½ cup sliced black olives
6 thinly sliced radishes
6 Tbsp olive oil
3 Tbsp red wine vinegar
1 tsp salt
Ground black pepper
¼ tsp dry mustard
1 clove garlic, minced
2 tomatoes cut into wedges
½ cup feta cheese, crumbled
2 Tbsp pine nuts, toasted

Cut the broccoli into florets. Drop them into a pot of boiling water for one minute, to blanch them. (If you prefer, you can also leave the broccoli raw.) Dump the broccoli into a large bowl and add the olives and radishes.

Whisk together the olive oil, vinegar, salt, pepper, mustard and garlic. Toss with the vegetables and marinate for several hours in the refrigerator.

Before serving, toss with the tomato, feta cheese and pine nuts.

Baby spinach salad

Serves four as a starter salad

Grocery stores now sell baby spinach pre-washed, and it's great to use as salad. I find that baby spinach holds up better than the mixed greens, although you can use any greens for this recipe.. This salad turns out surprisingly elegant and delicious. The trick to the salad is the pecans, which add an indescribably sweet and crunchy element. If you don't care for blue cheese, you can also use feta.

1 lemon
¼ cup olive oil
Pinch of cayenne pepper
Big pinch of salt

4 cups baby spinach
½ red onion, thinly sliced
¼ cup crumbled blue cheese
¼ cup dried cranberries
¼ cup pecans

In the bottom of the bowl in which you intend to serve the salad, whisk together the juice of the lemon, cayenne and salt, and then slowly whisk in the olive oil. Add the spinach and red onion and toss with the dressing. Add the blue cheese and cranberries.

In a toaster oven or a dry pan on the stovetop, lightly toast the pecans. Be careful not to burn them. Distribute them over the top and serve.

SALADS AND DRESSINGS: I often whisk the dressing right into the bottom of the salad bowl, pile my salad ingredients in, and toss everything together. However, with a salad that involves greens, it will get soggy if you leave it lying around for a while dressed. If you don't plan on serving it immediately, whisk the dressing together in a separate container and toss with the salad at the last minute.

Arugula salad with shaved parmesan

Serves four as a starter salad

Please use the absolute best Parmesan cheese you can find in this salad. It is expensive, but a little goes a long way, and the stuff will last for weeks in your fridge. Good Parmesan cheese bears no resemblance to the grated stuff you buy in canisters.

1½ Tbsp white wine vinegar
4 Tbsp olive oil
Salt and pepper
4 cups arugula, or any combination of greens, washed and dried, with large stems removed
2 small tomatoes, diced
1 large or 2 small red peppers, roasted
1 hunk of Parmesan cheese

In the bottom of the bowl in which you want to serve the salad, whisk together the white wine vinegar, olive oil, salt and pepper.

Right before serving, toss the greens with the dressing. Scatter the tomatoes on top, and then lay some strips of roasted pepper on top. Finally, using a vegetable peeler, shave slices of Parmesan over the top and serve.

Guacamole

When avocados are ripe, it just doesn't get any better than this.

- 3 ripe avocados
- 1 small tomato, diced (I squeeze the seeds out first)
- ⅓ cup diced red onion
- 1 clove garlic, smashed and minced
- 1 lime
- Generous handful of chopped cilantro (If you don't like cilantro, leave it out)
- Salt
- Black pepper
- Pinch of cayenne pepper

Mix everything together, and serve with chips.

ON AVOCADOS: When are avocados ripe? California avocados are the ones that look like they are encased in crocodile skin. The avocado is ripe when it is dark brown, and it gives ever so slightly when squeezed. Inside, the avocado should be light green, without any brown spots. There is a giant pit in the middle of the fruit, so run a knife around the circumference of the avocado, then twist the halves of the fruit and pull. Dislodge the pit, then use a big spoon to scoop out the flesh and cut it into cubes. In the alternative, you can use a knife to slice hashmarks into the avocado flesh while it is still in the skin, and then scoop out the cubed avocado. Avocado will turn brown once it is cut, so add a bit of lemon juice or lime juice on the surface of any avocado that you are not using. You can also place plastic wrap directly on the flesh of the cut half of an avocado to store it without it browning.

Salsa

Makes about 2 cups of salsa

I'm not opposed to buying salsa in jars, but it's so easy to make the stuff, and it tastes fresher than anything you can buy. You can get creative with this recipe and throw in any herbs or ingredients you like. As always, use as much or as little jalapeño as you like.

4 large ripe tomatoes
1 small red onion
2 scallions
1-2 limes, juiced
1 jalapeño, minced
Handful of cilantro, chopped (if you don't like cilantro, leave it out)
Pinch of salt and a few grinds of pepper

Cut the tomatoes in half and squeeze out the seeds for a drier salsa, or leave the seeds for a wetter one. Dice and put them in a bowl. Sprinkle the tomatoes with salt. (It helps release the juices and make it more liquid-y and therefore salsa-y). Dice up the red onion, mince the jalapeño, and thinly slice the scallions and add to the tomatoes. Stir in the lime juice and serve.

Parmesan roasted asparagus with eggs

Serves four as a starter or two for brunch

This is a great first course or brunch dish, and a really easy and tasty way to make asparagus. You can also skip the eggs and just roast the asparagus to serve it as a side dish. I can eat this for dinner, along with a good piece of bread to soak up all the eggy goodness.

1 bunch of asparagus
1½ Tbs olive oil
salt and pepper
2 Tbs grated parmesan cheese (the good stuff, please)
4 eggs
2 Tbs butter

Preheat oven to 400 degrees. Trim the woody ends off the asparagus. Put them on a cookie sheet and toss them with the olive oil, salt and pepper and parmesan cheese. Roast them in the oven until they are slightly brown, about 10 minutes.

While the asparagus is roasting, melt butter in a pan on low heat. Add the eggs, being careful not to break the yolks, and cook them until the whites are set and they are sunny side up, about 3 minutes.

Put the asparagus onto plates, and top with the eggs. Sprinkle the eggs with salt and pepper and serve.

Chicken and Meat

NO BONES ABOUT IT: This chapter has a chicken recipe for just about everybody. I've also included a couple of pork and meat recipes that use some of the cheaper cuts available. I know that when faced with the task of cooking dinner, sometimes the prospect of dealing with bones and skin is more than a body can stand—as a result, I use only boneless and skinless cuts of meat.

Chicken with ginger scallion sauce

Serves four

I probably make this dish once a week in the summer, because the sauce doesn't have to cook, and it's a snap to mix together. Simply cook the chicken and serve it with rice and the sauce. As for vegetables, I like broccoli here, but feel free to use carrots, zucchini, bok choy, or any combination of vegetables that you like.

1½ pounds chicken breasts (about 4 breasts)
½ cup water
¾ cup vegetable oil
¼ cup soy sauce
1/3 cup minced scallion
3 Tbsp grated ginger root
2 tsp toasted sesame oil
1 tsp hot chili oil
1 pound of vegetables, any kind
¾ cup + 2 Tbsp vegetable oil

Mix together the vegetable oil, soy sauce, scallion, ginger, sesame oil, and chili oil. You can make the sauce ahead of time, and it will keep for up to a week in the refrigerator.

Add another tablespoon of oil to a large pan. Add the chicken breasts and saute until they are cooked through, about 5–10 minutes per side, depending on the thickness of the chicken.

After the chicken is cooked, remove it to a plate and cover it to keep warm. Then, saute the vegetables in the same pan; if you are using something like broccoli, it will only take 2–3 minutes for it to cook through.

Serve with rice on a big platter, with the sauce in a bowl on the side to spoon over everything.

Cornmeal crusted chicken with arugula salad

Serves two, with leftovers

In this recipe, the cornmeal is a quick way to give the chicken a bit of a crispy crust. The brown sugar and cayenne pepper give the chicken a sweet-spicy flavor, which works really well with the pepperiness of the arugula and the buttery-ness of the avocado. As always, the cayenne pepper is to taste, and you can use whatever greens you like.

1½ pounds chicken breasts (about 4 breasts)
1 cup cornmeal
1½ Tbsp brown sugar
¼ tsp cayenne pepper, or to taste
Salt
3 Tbsp olive oil

1 large bunch of arugula
2 medium tomatoes
1 small red onion
½ avocado
2 Tbsp lemon juice
4 Tbsp olive oil
Salt and pepper

Pound the chicken breasts until they are flat and of uniform thickness. I usually cut the chicken in half, width-wise, then place the chicken breasts between two sheets of plastic wrap and whack them with a rolling pin until they are flat.

Heat the olive oil in a pan on medium high heat. Combine the cornmeal, brown sugar, cayenne pepper and a big pinch of salt on a plate. Dredge the chicken breasts in the cornmeal mixture and sauté until golden on each side, about 5 minutes per side. (You might need to cook the chicken in batches.)

Squeeze the seeds out of the tomatoes and chop them. Chop the red onion and dice the avocado. Coarsely chop the arugula, and combine all of the vegetables. In a small bowl or jelly jar, squeeze the juice of the lemon, add a generous pinch of salt and pepper, then whisk in the olive oil. Dress the salad lightly, then pile the salad on top of the chicken breasts and serve.

Chili

Serves two with leftovers

On a cold night, I sometimes crave chili, but I've spent the day working, instead of staying home and babysitting a simmering pot of chili. This recipe can be made in about 30 minutes — I think that it's much better than the store-bought stuff.

1½ pounds ground beef
1 can red kidney beans, drained
3 Tbsp olive oil
1½ Tbsp chili powder
1½ Tbsp cumin
1 Tbsp cocoa powder
1 tsp coriander
1 tsp cinnamon
1 tsp salt
2 tsp sugar
3 cloves of garlic, chopped
1 medium onion, chopped
2 Tbsp cider vinegar
3 Tbsp tomato paste
1½ cups water
Scallions (optional)
Grated cheddar cheese (optional)
Sour cream (optional)
Cilantro (optional)
Pickled jalapeños (very optional)

Heat the olive oil in a large pan over low heat. Sauté the cumin, coriander, cocoa, chili powder, garlic, salt and sugar until it slightly darkens in color and smells fragrant, about 3–5 minutes. Add the chopped onion and cook until the onion is soft, another 5 minutes. Add the tomato paste and let it toast for 2 minutes. Add the beef and cook until it is brown, about 5 minutes. Drain the kidney beans and add them to the chili. Add the water and the cider vinegar, bring to a boil and simmer for about 10 minutes, until thick, then serve.

Serve with sour cream, cheddar cheese, scallions and cilantro, or whatever toppings you like. I love pickled jalapeños in this chili, but then I pretty much love pickled jalapeños in everything I eat…

Chicken piccata

Serves two people, with leftovers

If I have some chicken in the refrigerator and I can't decide what to do with it, this is usually what I do. You can skip pounding the chicken, but I find that it cooks more evenly that way. Serve it with pasta or potatoes.

1½ pounds chicken breasts (about 4 breasts)
1 cup flour
Salt and pepper
1 lemon
3 Tbsp butter
2 Tbsp olive oil
½ cup white wine
½ cup chicken stock (canned is fine)
1½ Tbsp capers
Handful of flat leaf parsley, chopped

Pound the chicken breasts until they are flat and of uniform thickness. Place the flour, salt and pepper on a plate. Dredge each chicken breast in the flour mixture.

Heat the oil and a tablespoon of the butter in a pan until hot. Brown the chicken on both sides in the hot pan, about 6 minutes per side, and remove it to a plate. Cover the chicken with foil to keep it warm.

After the chicken is removed from the pan, reduce the heat to low. Pour in the white wine, using a wooden spoon to scrape up the bits from the bottom of the pan. Add the juice of the lemon and the capers. Throw in the rest of the butter and stir together the sauce. Put the chicken back in, throw the parsley on top, and serve.

Chicken with mango salsa and coconut rice

Serves two, with leftovers

This is a terrific dish, but it tastes the best in spring and summer, when mangos are ripe. The shredded coconut is optional; if you do use it, be careful to use unsweetened coconut.

- 1 cup jasmine rice
- Salt
- 1 cup coconut milk (light coconut milk works fine)
- 3 Tbsp unsweetened shredded coconut (optional)
- 1½ Tbsp soy sauce
- Tobasco sauce, to taste (5–10 shakes should do the trick)
- 1 Tbsp honey
- 1½ Tbsp olive oil
- 1½ pounds chicken breasts
- 2 mangos (I like the yellow champagne mangos, when I can find them)
- 1 small red onion
- 1 small red pepper
- ½ small clove garlic, finely chopped
- Juice of 2 limes
- 1 jalapeño, chopped (optional for those who like heat)
- Bunch of cilantro, chopped

Put one cup of rice in a pot with some salt, one cup of water and one cup of coconut milk. Follow the instructions for cooking the rice; generally it takes 20 minutes to have perfect rice.

Toast the shredded coconut in a dry pan until golden brown, about 3 minutes, and mix with the cooked rice.

Mix the soy sauce, juice of one lime, honey, Tabasco and olive oil in a plastic bag, and let the chicken marinate in it for 20 minutes to 1 hour. Don't let it marinate too long, or the lime juice will start to cook the chicken.

Chop the mangos, red onion and red pepper and mix together in a bowl. Add the garlic and the juice of the other lime. If you are using jalapeño, add that as well. Add the chopped cilantro and mix well.

Remove the chicken from the marinade and broil it under a hot broiler until it is brown on top and just cooked through, about 8–12 minutes per side (depending on the thickness of the chicken). Top with the mango salsa, and serve with coconut rice.

Mustard-soy glazed chicken

Serves two, with leftovers

Here's a little known fact: soy sauce tenderizes meat. I let the chicken marinate all day, or even overnight, and the flavor is great. I make this dish all the time because it is just so easy and quick, and all the components (except, of course, the chicken) keep in the pantry.

2 Tbsp Dijon mustard
2 Tbsp soy sauce
2 Tbsp olive oil
2 cloves of garlic, finely minced
Salt and pepper to taste
1½ pounds chicken breasts

Mix together all the ingredients except the chicken in a plastic bag. Reserve a few spoonfuls of the mustard mixture. Add the chicken to the remainder of the mustard mixture and marinate anywhere from 10 minutes to a day.

You can either broil the chicken or grill it in a grill pan. It takes about 8–12 minutes per side to broil the chicken. Serve each breast topped with a little of the reserved mustard, along with salad and a baguette.

ON BROILERS: If you are nervous to use your broiler it is helpful to consider that a broiler is basically an upside-down grill, with the heat source above the food, rather than below it. Which is why it makes such a good substitute, if you don't happen to have a barbecue. I usually broil the food about 6 inches from the heat source, so my broiling times are based on that distance. I also have the option of broiling under high or low heat, and I usually broil chicken on low heat. You may have to adjust the cooking times based on the broiler that you have. If it takes longer for the food to cook (or you accidentally burn something), don't give up! You'll get the hang of it.

Chicken with mushrooms

Serves two, with leftovers

This is one of those reliable recipes. It always tastes great, it's easy, and it's a crowd pleaser. I really like the combination of sherry vinegar and mushrooms, but you can use any vinegar you have on hand. If you happen to have dry sherry, you can use that as well.

- 3 Tbsp olive oil
- 1½ pounds chicken breasts
- Salt and pepper to taste
- 1 cup flour
- 12 button mushrooms, cleaned and sliced
- 2 Tbsp sherry vinegar
- ½ cup canned chicken stock (you can also use water)
- 2 Tbsp butter
- 3 Tbsp chopped flat leaf Italian parsley

Heat the olive oil in a sauté pan big enough to hold the chicken.

Pound the chicken breasts until they are of uniform thickness. Mix a big pinch of salt and some black pepper with the flour on a plate. Dredge each chicken breast in the flour, then sauté over high heat until brown on both sides, about 6 minutes per side.

Remove the chicken to a plate and cover it with foil to keep it warm. Put the sliced mushrooms in the same pan and sauté over high heat until the mushrooms have released their liquid and browned. Add the sherry vinegar and chicken stock and simmer until the sauce thickens and reduces a little, about 3–5 minutes. Swirl in the butter. Add back the chicken, warm it up for a minute, add the parsley and serve.

Roast chicken

Serves four

Okay, okay. I know I said I don't cook with skin and bones, but this dish is REALLY good and really easy. By putting the butter and herbs under the skin, the meat stays moist as the butter moves through it, leaving the herbs to flavor the meat on top. I use whole chicken breasts in this dish, but you can use whatever you like best. You can also alter the herbs in the dish and use rosemary or thyme or anything you prefer instead of dill.

4 Tbsp butter, softened
2 Tbsp dill, finely chopped
2 Tbsp flat leaf Italian parsley, finely chopped
1 clove of garlic, finely minced
Salt and pepper to taste
4 chicken breasts with the bone in and skin on, (about 2½ pounds)

In a small bowl, mix together the softened butter, dill, parsley, garlic and a sprinkle of salt and pepper until combined.

Wash the chicken breasts and pat dry. Loosen the skin from the top of each breast. Using your fingers, spread some of the butter under the skin and directly onto the breast meat until it evenly coats. Sprinkle salt and pepper on the top of each breast. Roast in the oven, on a rack if you have one, at 400 degrees until the skin is crispy and brown and the juices run clear, about 35–45 minutes. Serve with a vegetable of your choice; a personal favorite is wilted greens sautéed in olive oil with some garlic and red pepper flakes.

NOTE: I use chicken breasts with the skin on and the bone in for this recipe, but you can certainly use a whole chicken, cut into pieces, or chicken thighs with the bone in and skin on. You will have to vary the cooking times slightly, depending on which cuts of chicken you use.

Middle Eastern spiced chicken

Serves two, with leftovers

This is yet another quick and easy way to broil chicken, one that benefits from sitting in the refrigerator all day in its marinade. The yogurt makes the chicken incredibly tender, and the flavors of the spices really get into the meat. When the weather gets hot, try this one with Summer Couscous.

1 Tbsp cumin
1 Tbsp coriander
1 tsp turmeric
1 tsp cinnamon
2 cloves garlic, chopped
1½ pounds chicken breasts
1 cup plain yogurt (I like Greek yogurt)
1 lemon
2 Tbsp olive oil
1 tsp salt
Black pepper to taste

Combine all the spices, the garlic, salt, pepper and yogurt in a plastic bag. Squeeze the juice of the lemon into the bag, and add the olive oil. Throw in the chicken breasts, and mush everything around in the bag until each breast is well coated.

Broil until the chicken is cooked through, 8–12 minutes per side.

Pork tenderloin with mustard-apricot glaze

Serves two, with leftovers

This one is a crowd pleaser. The apricot jam gives the whole dish a little twist of sweet and fruit that goes great with the pork and the mustard. You can serve this with plain rice and broccoli with lemon-garlic vinaigrette.

2 lbs pork tenderloin
Salt and pepper
2 Tbsp peanut oil

2 Tbsp mustard
3 Tbsp soy sauce
2 Tbsp rice vinegar
1 Tbsp apricot jam
1 clove garlic, chopped
Hot red pepper flakes

Preheat oven to 400 degrees.

Season the pork tenderloin all around with salt and pepper. Heat peanut oil in a pan until hot, and sear the tenderloin on the stovetop until all sides are brown. Roast in the oven until the pork is medium rare (when a meat thermometer reads 145 degrees), about 10–15 minutes.

Whisk together the mustard, soy, rice vinegar, apricot jam, garlic and hot pepper in a bowl. Spoon the glaze over the top and sides of the tenderloin while it is still hot. Let the meat rest for 10 minutes before slicing and serving.

Asian marinated flank steak

Serve over rice, if you like, with the reserved sauce

I like to throw a flank steak into the marinade in the morning before work, and then broil it when I get home, but you definitely don't need to marinate it for twelve hours for the meat to taste great. You will get great flavor from marinating in as little as 20 minutes.

1½ pounds flank steak
2 cloves garlic, chopped
3 scallions, white and green parts sliced
¼ cup soy sauce
2 Tbsp rice vinegar
1 Tbsp sesame oil
Several shakes of Tabasco, or any other hot sauce

In a small bowl, mix together all of the ingredients except the steak. Line a roasting pan with aluminum foil, add the steak, and pour about half the soy mixture over the steak, turning to coat. (Reserve the other half of the sauce for serving.) Let marinate for anywhere between 20 minutes and 12 hours.

Broil the steak until medium rare, about 8–10 minutes per side. Let the steak rest for about 10 minutes before slicing it thin, against the grain.

Beef tenderloin with horseradish sauce

Serves two with leftovers (if you're lucky)

Tenderloin is normally quite expensive, but when it's on sale at my grocery store I snap it up. This recipe is ridiculously easy, and the results are awesome. The raw steak freezes well, too, so you can buy it on sale, and then defrost it to really impress dinner guests.

1–1½ pounds beef tenderloin, trimmed and tied
1 Tbsp olive oil
Salt and pepper

For the horseradish sauce:
1/3 cup sour cream
1 Tbsp Dijon mustard
1 Tbsp prepared horseradish (or more, to taste)
1 Tbsp lemon juice
1 Tbsp chopped chives
Salt and pepper

Preheat the oven to 450 degrees. Allow the meat to come to room temperature, and then pat it dry with paper towels. Rub the olive oil on all sides of the meat, and then season all sides of the meat with salt and pepper. (Be generous with the seasoning.)

Heat an oven-proof pan on high heat, and then add the meat. Sear it on all sides until it is brown. (This should take about 5 minutes per side.) Put the pan in the oven until the steak is rare to medium-rare, about 10–15 minutes, depending on the thickness of the meat. Allow the meat to rest for at least 10 minutes.

Meanwhile, make the horseradish sauce by mixing all the ingredients together.

Slice the steak and serve with the horseradish sauce on the side.

Beef brisket with horseradish

Serves 8 to 10 people

Brisket takes hours to cook, but the good news is that you really don't have to do anything that whole time, and at the end you have something really delicious. Don't be put off by the amount of garlic in this recipe. When the whole cloves cook, they get nutty and mild, and flavor the beef really well. As for the horseradish, it's an unusual ingredient here, but I'll never make another brisket without it.

2 Tbs olive oil
1 beef brisket (about 5 pounds) patted dry
salt and pepper
40 cloves of garlic, peeled (you can buy peeled garlic cloves)
¼ cup balsamic vinegar or red wine
3 cups beef or chicken broth
2 Tbs prepared horseradish

Sprinkle both sides of the brisket with lots of salt and pepper.

Preheat oven to 325 degrees.

Heat a large, ovenproof pot or pan big enough to hold the brisket over medium-high heat. Add olive oil, and then the brisket, fat side down. Sear it until it is brown, then flip it over and sear the other side. After both sides are brown, remove it to a plate. Add garlic to the pan and stir until the garlic begins to turn golden. Add the balsamic vinegar and stir up the browned bits at the bottom of the pan. Add the beef or chicken broth, then turn off the heat and add back the brisket. Cover it tightly and put it in the oven.

Bake the brisket at 325 degrees for 1 hour. Reduce the heat to 300 degrees and bake for another 1½ to 2 hours. Then remove the brisket to a plate and cover it to keep them warm. Using a potato masher, mash the garlic cloves into the gravy until it is smooth. Stir the horseradish into the gravy.

Cut the meat against the grain into slices (it will still be pretty hard). Then return the slices to the gravy and cook for another hour, until the meat is fork tender.

Fish and Seafood

AT SEA: Afraid of buying mussels? Terrified of hidden salmon bones? Don't be. Fish fillets like salmon and cod can be found pretty inexpensively, and if you buy the fillet, rest assured that the bones have been removed. (You can also press your fingers along the flesh of the fish: you will feel any bones that are left.) And if you're not aware of this already, cultivated mussels cost only a couple of dollars per pound. Even better, since they are cultivated they don't have long, scary beards or require much cleaning beyond a rinse under cold water.

Salmon with bread crumb-dill crust

Serves two

Salmon, lemon and dill go really well together. Serve with a nice salad and a good hunk of bread. As a bonus, this dish looks really nice coming out of the oven, and you can easily impress a crowd

3 Tbsp fresh dill, chopped
1 cup bread crumbs (preferably fresh, but can use panko in a pinch)
Salt and pepper
Two lemons
2–3 Tbsp olive oil
1 Tbsp Dijon mustard
1 pound fillets of salmon

Preheat the oven to 375 degrees. If you are using fresh breadcrumbs, toast them in the oven until they are just brown, 5–8 minutes. Remove the rind of the lemons with a grater. Mince the dill and toss with lemon rind, bread crumbs, salt and pepper. Mix the olive oil into the bread crumb mixture until everything is moist. Smear the mustard over the flesh of the salmon, squeeze the juice of the lemon over the mustard coating, and then pack the bread crumb mixture on top.

Bake the salmon until it is medium rare, about 12–18 minutes. If the bread crumbs are not crispy and brown, broil the salmon for about 30 seconds. Serve.

NOTE: Watch the salmon very carefully when under the broiler, because it burns very easily. Thirty seconds is literally all the time it needs to brown.

Salmon with soy sauce

Serves two

This is another of my mom's recipes. She has often served crowds with this dish, and people love it, never realizing how easy it is.

⅓ cup soy sauce
3 scallions, sliced
1 Tbsp grated ginger
2 cloves of garlic, chopped
1 tsp sugar
1 pound salmon

Combine the soy sauce, scallions, ginger and garlic in a plastic bag. Add the salmon and let it marinate for as much time as you have. When you are ready to cook, remove the fish from the marinade and broil the fish until it is cooked through and the top is mahogany in color, about 8–12 minutes. Meanwhile, pour the sauce into a small pot, add the sugar and boil until the sauce is somewhat thickened and reduced, 5–10 minutes. Pour the sauce over the salmon and serve.

ON GINGER: Ginger is such a delicious flavor, simultaneously spicy and sweet. Its texture, however, is less worthy of rapture because ginger, especially older ginger root, is very fibrous. Look for ginger root where the skin is tight and unwrinkled. Peel the skin with a small spoon, and then grate the flesh as finely as possible to get all the flavor, without the fiber.

Tilapia with orange and chili

Serves two

This is my idea of a perfect recipe: it's quick to make, it's healthy to eat, and it tastes absolutely delicious. Alter the jalapeño pepper to suit your taste.

1 cup flour
1 tsp chili powder
1 tsp cumin
1 tsp salt
One orange
1 whole jalapeño
1 Tbsp olive oil
2 Tbsp butter
1 pound tilapia fillets
3 Tbsp cider vinegar

Remove the rind of the orange with a grater. Combine flour with 1 tsp chili powder, the cumin, salt and the grated rind of the orange. Thinly slice the jalapeño pepper and set aside.

Heat the olive oil and half the butter in a large skillet. Dredge the fish in the flour mixture and shake off the excess. Sauté the fish on each side until golden, about 3–4 minutes per side. If the fish starts to burn, add a bit more oil or butter.

After the fish is golden on both sides, remove and put on a dish, cover with foil and keep warm. Add the sliced chili and sauté for a minute. Squeeze the juice of the orange into the pan, add the vinegar, and use a wooden spoon to get up the little bits. If the sauce gets too dry, add a little more vinegar or water. Add the rest of the butter to finish the sauce. Return the fish to the pan, and heat through, and then serve.

Mussels in white wine

Serves four as an appetizer, two as a main dish

I love this dish. You might never order mussels in a restaurant again....

2 Tbsp olive oil
3 cloves of garlic, chopped
1 shallot, chopped
Red pepper flakes
1½ pounds mussels, scrubbed
Salt
1 cup white wine
2 Tbsp butter
Handful of flat leaf Italian parsley, chopped

Heat olive oil in a pan large enough to hold the mussels. Add garlic, shallot and red pepper flakes, and sauté on low heat until soft, about 2–4 minutes. (Don't burn the garlic.) Add the mussels, season with salt, then pour in the cup of wine and close the lid. Cook until the mussels open, about 5–10 minutes. Add the butter and shake the pan around to distribute it as it melts. Sprinkle the parsley over the top and serve with lots of bread for dunking.

Mussels marinara

Serves two

This is a classic recipe, and the best part is that it's so easy to make. If you buy tubes of tomato paste and anchovy paste, they will keep for quite a while in your refrigerator. The only part of this recipe that you can't store is the mussels.

2 Tbsp olive oil
4 cloves garlic, chopped
1 Tbsp anchovy paste
½ tsp red pepper flakes
1 Tbsp tomato paste
¾ cup white wine
1-28 oz can crushed tomato
½ pound pasta
1½ pounds mussels, scrubbed
Flat leaf Italian parsley, chopped

Cook the pasta.

Add the olive oil to a large pan under medium-low heat. Add the garlic, along with the anchovy paste and red pepper flakes. Cook until the ingredients melt together, about 3 minutes. Add the tomato paste and cook until you can smell the tomato and it slightly darkens in color, about another 3 minutes. Add the wine and cook for 2 minutes. Add the tomatoes, bring to a boil, and simmer on low heat for 15 minutes.

Cook the pasta. Five minutes before the pasta is done, throw the mussels into the sauce and put the lid back on the pan. After the pasta is drained, put it in a bowl, put the sauce over the pasta, sprinkle with the parsley and serve.

Garlic shrimp

Serves two

Serve this one with lots of crusty bread for dunking. I like this with the Mediterranean chopped salad. If you want to dress it up, serve some roasted peppers, sautéed mushrooms, olives, Manchego cheese and slices of Serrano ham to make it a real Spanish tapas dinner.

¼ cup olive oil
4 cloves garlic, thinly sliced
1 Tbsp cumin
1 Tbsp paprika
½ tsp cayenne pepper
1 lb large shrimp, peeled and deveined
½ cup white wine
Flat leaf Italian parsley, chopped

Heat the oil in a sauté pan along with the garlic slices over low heat. When the garlic just starts to get fragrant and turn slightly golden, about one minute, then add the cumin, paprika and cayenne and let the spices sauté. After a couple of minutes, add the shrimp and the wine and raise the heat to medium. When the wine is bubbling and the shrimp is pink, sprinkle with parsley and serve.

ON SHRIMP: I hate deveining shrimp and I'm too cheap to buy shrimp already deveined. But when you're considering the size shrimp you want to buy, remember that the bigger the shrimp, the fewer there will be per pound, and the fewer, therefore, that you will have to devein.

Fish with gremolata

Serves two

This one is barely even a recipe, but it's a great way to serve fish. Gremolata is a classic mixture of garlic, lemon and parsley and is typically served with beef, but I love it with fish. Any firm, white fleshed fish will work well with this recipe. Gremolata is really nothing but a solid flavor punch, so a little goes a long way….

1 pound of thick, white fish fillets (like cod)
1 lemon
¼ cup parsley, chopped
3 cloves garlic, finely minced
4 Tbsp olive oil
Salt and pepper

Preheat the oven to 375 degrees. Remove the zest of the lemon with a grater. Mix the zest with the parsley, garlic, juice of half the lemon and 3 Tbsp of olive oil. Season with salt and pepper.

Season the fish with salt and pepper, and juice the other half of the lemon over the fish fillets. Drizzle with a bit of olive oil. Roast the fish in the oven until cooked through, about 12–18 minutes, depending on the thickness of the fish. (You can also cook the fish in a pan on the stove, or under a broiler.) Top with the gremolata and serve.

Mexican spicy shrimp

Serves two

This yummy shrimp dish is light, yet spicy and substantial. Don't be put off by the number of ingredients—but if you feel overwhelmed, you can cheat by substituting store-bought salsa for the tomatoes, onions and spices. Serve with rice.

3 Tbsp olive oil
2 cloves garlic, chopped
1 jalapeño, chopped (or to taste)
½ tsp coriander
½ tsp chili powder
1 medium yellow onion, chopped
1½ pounds tomatoes, chopped
½ tsp oregano
Juice of 1 lime
1 tsp salt
1 pound shrimp, peeled and deveined
3 scallions, sliced
Handful of cilantro, chopped

Cook the rice according to the package. (It is usually 1 cup of rice to 2 cups of water.)

Heat the olive oil in a skillet over medium heat. Add the garlic, jalapeño, coriander, chili powder and red pepper flakes and cook until fragrant, about 1–2 minutes. Add the onions and sauté until they are soft, about 5 minutes.

Add the tomatoes, the salt and the lime juice and cook until the tomatoes are very soft, about 10–15 minutes. If the sauce looks too dry, add some water. Add the shrimp, cover the pan and cook for 3–5 minutes, until the shrimp are pink.

When the shrimp are cooked, sprinkle the scallion and cilantro over the shrimp. Serve over rice.

Old Bay fish with cucumber dill sauce

Serves two with leftovers

I like to use cod for this recipe, but you can really use any fish that looks good or is on sale. The cucumber dill sauce is delicious with the spicy fish, but it's also great as a dip.

1 pound thick fish fillets, like cod
¾ cup fresh bread crumbs or panko
¾ cup buttermilk
2½ Tbs Old Bay seasoning
½ tsp garlic powder
½ tsp cayenne pepper (optional, if you want more spice than from the Old Bay)
Salt
2 Tbs oil

⅓ cup plain yogurt (use the thick Greek yogurt)
½ small English cucumber
1 Tbs dill, finely chopped
1 Tbs scallions, finely chopped
salt and pepper to taste

Preheat the oven to 375 degrees. Peel the cucumber, then slice it in half lengthwise. Use a small spoon to scoop out the seeds. Finely grate the cucumber halves on a box grater, then squeeze out as much water as you can. You should wind up with about ¼ cup of cucumber. Put the cucumber in a bowl and season with some salt. Then mix in the yogurt, dill and scallions. Add some salt and pepper to taste.

Mix together the bread crumbs or panko with the Old Bay, garlic powder, salt, and cayenne, (if you are using it). Dip the fish in the buttermilk until it is coated, then dredge the fish in the bread crumb mixture. Bake until the fish is cooked through and the bread crumbs are browned, about 12–18 minutes.

Serve the fish with a dollop of sauce on top, and more on the side.

Pasta

PASTA: I love pasta. Who doesn't? But even when you're scrambling to put dinner on the table, there's no reason to reach for the jar of sauce. This chapter includes lots of delicious sauces that go way beyond a simple marinara. Give them a try—you may find some tasty and easy alternatives to what you find in a bottle.

Pasta carbonara plus

Serves two

I've always loved pasta carbonara, which is basically pasta with bacon and eggs, but I thought that there was probably a way to lighten it up a little and actually make the dish better. Here's what I came up with. I kept all the yummy ingredients, but I've added spinach and tomatoes, to make it a one-dish supper.

5 slices of bacon, chopped
1 yellow onion, finely chopped
Large handful of grape tomatoes, halved
Salt
Lots of freshly ground black pepper
½ pound long pasta like linguine
1 cup pasta cooking water
1 package baby spinach, coarsely chopped
2 eggs
½ cup freshly grated best-quality Parmesan cheese

Cook the pasta, reserving 1 cup of the pasta cooking water.

In a large pan, cook the bacon over medium high heat. When the bacon is crisp, drain all but one tablespoon of the fat, add the onion and lower the heat. Cook until the onion starts to soften and look translucent, about 3–5 minutes. Add the tomatoes, along with some salt and pepper. Turn the heat to low.

Toss the cooked pasta and the spinach into the pan with the bacon, onion and tomato and toss with tongs until coated. Take the pan off the heat, crack in both eggs and toss. (If it's dry, add a little of the pasta water.) Lastly, toss in the cheese and some more pepper and serve.

Spicy shrimp with linguine

Serves two

As the title of the recipe suggests, this recipe is for fellow chili lovers. It calls for cherry peppers, which are packed in vinegar and deliver a little acidic kick, along with some heat. Once the shrimp are peeled and deveined (an admittedly annoying task), you can make the sauce in the time it takes for the pasta to cook.

¾ pound linguine
4 Tbsp olive oil
1 pound shrimp, peeled and deveined
Salt and pepper
3–5 cherry peppers, sliced
1 red pepper, sliced
5–6 cloves of garlic, chopped
½ cup white wine
1 Tbsp tomato paste
¼–½ cup pasta cooking water
3 Tbsp cream
½ cup chopped parsley

Cook the pasta, reserving 1 cup of the pasta cooking water.

Heat a large skillet over medium high heat. Add 2 Tbsp of olive oil, and then add the shrimp in a single layer. Season with salt and pepper, and sauté the shrimp until they are just pink, 2–3 minutes per side. Remove the shrimp to a plate and cover with foil to keep warm.

Reduce the heat to low and add the rest of the olive oil. Add the cherry peppers, bell pepper, and garlic. Sauté until fragrant, about 2 minutes, then add wine and tomato paste. Simmer for 3–5 minutes. If the sauce gets too dry, add a splash of the pasta cooking water. Add the cream, season with salt and pepper, toss the shrimp back in, add the pasta, toss everything together for 1–2 minutes, sprinkle with parsley and serve.

Tortellini with eggplant puree

Serves four, with extra sauce

Okay, okay, I said I wouldn't use a food processor in any of my recipes. But this one is so good, and unusual, that I thought I would throw it in here. You can use a blender instead of a food processor, or even just chop all the vegetables as fine as you can for a somewhat chunkier, but still tasty, sauce. I like this best with cheese tortellini. This sauce also freezes really well.

2½ cups of eggplant, peeled and diced
2 cloves of garlic
1 onion
Olive oil for the pan
Salt and pepper
⅓ cup grated best-quality Parmesan
1 handful of basil leaves
1–1½ cups water
1 8 oz can of tomato sauce
1½ pounds tortellini

Peel the eggplant, and cut into cubes. Slice the garlic. Cut the onion into a rough chop. Put some olive oil in the bottom of the skillet, and sauté the eggplant, garlic and onion with a pinch of salt until the vegetables are soft, about 10 minutes. Let the vegetables cool slightly.

Dump the vegetables, the Parmesan and the basil leaves in the bowl of a food processor or blender. (If you use a blender you might need to do it in batches.) Run the machine and puree, adding some water to get it to a sauce-like consistency. (This will take approximately 1 cup of water, depending on how thick you want the sauce.) Dump it back into the pan, add the can of tomato sauce, and warm it through.

Cook the tortellini. Once it is al dente, toss the tortellini with some of the pasta and serve.

Orzo with wild mushrooms

Serves four as a side dish or two as a main course

This can be a side dish or, with a salad, a meal unto itself. Please don't leave out the dried mushrooms! Although they can be expensive, they add tons of flavor, and a little goes a long way. I like to use dried Porcini mushrooms, but any dried mushroom will work.

¾ pound orzo
1 ounce dried mushrooms
1 pound fresh cremini mushrooms
2 Tbsp olive oil
5 cloves of garlic, minced
2–3 Tbsp sherry
¼–½ cup reserved pasta cooking water
Parmesan cheese
Handful of Italian parsley, chopped

Cook the pasta, reserving 1 cup of the pasta cooking water.

Soak dried mushrooms in 1 cup of very hot water for about 20 minutes. DO NOT DISCARD THE SOAKING LIQUID! It has lots of flavor and will be added to the pasta. When the mushrooms are soft, chop them.

Slice fresh mushrooms into 1/4 inch slices. Heat olive oil in a large skillet on medium high heat. Sauté the mushrooms until they release their liquid and brown, about 10 minutes. Lower the heat and add the garlic and the dried mushrooms. Cook just until the garlic becomes fragrant, and then add the sherry and the soaking liquid from the mushrooms. Be careful not to include the grit that inevitably drifts to the bottom of the soaking liquid.

Add the pasta and, if it looks dry, add some of the pasta cooking water. (I usually add a few splashes.) Toss everything together, add grated Parmesan cheese and parsley and serve.

NOTE: Do not skip the parsley! It adds brightness, flavor, and color, and is well worth the chopping time.

Vietnamese summer noodles

Serves four

One of the nice things about this recipe is that it uses rice vermicelli, which cooks by soaking in hot water. On a hot day, I like to eat a light pasta dish without boiling a massive pot of water to cook it. Any rice noodle will work here, or even regular pasta in a pinch. If you are using regular pasta, increase the amount to ¾ of a pound.

½ pound shrimp, peeled and deveined
½ pound ground pork
½ pound rice vermicelli
4 scallions, sliced
Handful of basil leaves, shredded
Handful of cilantro leaves, chopped
Handful of mint leaves, shredded
1 carrot, shredded
5 cloves of garlic, minced
1 tsp Sriracha, or other hot sauce, to taste
2 Tbsp vegetable oil
1 cucumber, cut into small matchsticks
4 Tbsp lime juice
2 Tbsp fish sauce
2 Tbsp rice vinegar
2 Tbsp sugar

Place vermicelli in a large bowl and pour hot water over the pasta until it is covered. Soak until pasta is pliable, about 5–10 minutes, then drain.

Dissolve the sugar in the lime juice in a large bowl. Mix in the fish sauce, the hot sauce and the rice vinegar. Add the carrot and 1 clove of minced garlic and set aside.

Heat the vegetable oil in a medium pan and sauté the rest of the garlic until it is fragrant, about one minute. Add the pork and cook until it is browned, about 3–5 minutes. Add the shrimp, and cook until the shrimp is just pink, another 3–5 minutes. Mix the shrimp, pork and rice vermicelli into the bowl with the sauce. Top with the herbs, scallions, lettuce and cucumber and serve.

ON FISH SAUCE: Please do not fear the fish sauce! Yes, it smells strange, and the ingredient list is terrifying—it's usually made from fermented anchovy—but fish sauce is one of the keys to making delicious Vietnamese food. It is sold in most grocery stores now, so just buy a bottle and try it. Live dangerously! You won't regret it.

Macaroni & cheese

Sure, it isn't the healthiest dish in the world, but sometimes there is nothing better. Macaroni & cheese never fails to cheer me up on a cold winter night.

1 lb macaroni, cooked al dente
4 Tbsp flour
4 Tbsp butter
4 cups whole milk
Dry mustard
Salt and pepper
1 tsp Tabasco
4 cups cheese
½ cup bread crumbs

Preheat the oven to 350 degrees. In a large pot, stir flour and butter together until it forms a light golden paste called a roux. Pour in the milk and add the spices. Whisk the milk into the flour-butter mixture until it is all the same consistency, and it thickens slightly, just a little thicker than heavy cream. Add the cooked macaroni and about half the cheese, and mix everything together.

Pour the macaroni into a small, deep casserole dish if you like your macaroni & cheese gooey inside, and into a shallow baking pan if you like it drier. Sprinkle the rest of the cheese on top, and the bread crumbs on top of that.

Bake in a 350 degree oven for 30 minutes in a shallow pan and one hour in a deep dish, until it is bubbling and the top is crunchy.

ON CHEESE: Of course, you can vary the cheese depending on your taste. If you tend to the old school, the only choice is cheddar, but I like using some gruyere mixed in—also, if you add some fontina cheese to the mix, the macaroni & cheese will be creamier.

Spaghetti and meatballs

Serve over spaghetti with cheese. Serves four

What can I say? Everyone's got her own meatball recipe, but if you're not completely happy with your meatballs, give these a try. You might want to double the recipe, because it freezes well. Most people recommend frying meatballs, but I just braise them in the tomato sauce. They stay incredibly moist that way, and it is much easier to simply drop the meatballs into a waiting pot of sauce than to individually fry the meatballs.

2 pound ground beef
2 eggs
½ cup bread crumbs
⅓ cup grated best-quality Parmesan cheese
1 tsp oregano
Salt and pepper
2 pinches red pepper flakes
3 Tbsp olive oil
4 cloves garlic, minced (divided)
1–28 oz can + 1–14 oz can of whole San Marzano plum tomatoes
1 can chicken stock
1 pound spaghetti or any type of pasta you favor

Cook the pasta.

In a large bowl, mix together eggs, bread crumbs, cheese, oregano, one chopped clove of garlic, salt and red pepper flakes. Add the meats and a splash of warm water (The water is very important! It helps keep the meatballs moist.) Use your hands to mush everything together until it is just mixed. Make the meatballs—I like mine to be about the size of golf balls. Wet your hands to prevent the meat from sticking.

Heat olive oil in a large pot on medium heat, along with the rest of the garlic and some crushed red pepper flakes. When the garlic is light gold and you can smell it, add the tomatoes and the chicken stock. Bring to a boil, then reduce it to a simmer. Drop in the meatballs and cook until the sauce slightly thickens and the meatballs are cooked through. I usually wait another half hour, but the meatballs will be cooked through before then.

Spaghetti with corn and tomatoes

Serves two with leftovers

Make this in the late summer, when tomatoes and corn are at their tastiest. I absolutely love the combination of grilled corn and raw tomatoes.

1 lb spaghetti
2 lbs tomatoes
¼ cup olive oil
Salt and crushed red pepper flakes
Handful of basil leaves, shredded
3 cloves of garlic
3 ears corn
Grated Parmesan cheese, to taste

Cook the pasta.

Meanwhile, coarsely chop the tomatoes and squeeze out the seeds. (Some people might like to peel the tomatoes first. I usually don't bother, but if you prefer skinless tomatoes, drop them in boiling water for 1 minute, and the peel will slide off. You can use the same pot of boiling water that you use to cook the spaghetti.) Put the chopped tomatoes in a large bowl with the olive oil and a generous sprinkling of salt and crushed red pepper flakes. Add the torn basil leaves. Whack the cloves of garlic with the flat of a knife to release their oils, and add them to the bowl. (If you really love garlic, as I do, finely mince one of the cloves and add that as well.)

While the tomatoes are marinating, place the ears of corn on a grill pan, rotating until there are some browned kernels on all sides. (This shouldn't take more than 2–3 minutes per side.) Cut the kernels off the cobs and add to the tomatoes.

When the spaghetti is ready, remove the whole garlic cloves from the sauce, toss in the pasta, and serve with plenty of Parmesan cheese.

Sesame noodles

Serves four with the chicken, two without

For some reason, there are a lot of bad sesame noodles out there. Not only bad tasting noodles, but noodles where the consistency is all wrong. This dish doesn't have that problem. The secret is the water, which helps loosen up the peanut butter and form the tasty sauce. The shredded chicken is optional, but if you do add it, you have a one-dish meal. I like the snow peas in this dish, but you could also shred carrot, or dice peppers, or add any other vegetables you have on hand.

½ pound pasta
4 Tbsp soy sauce
3 Tbsp rice vinegar
2 Tbsp toasted sesame oil
1 tsp chili oil (optional)
Pinch of salt
Crushed red pepper, to taste
3 Tbsp creamy peanut butter
⅓ cup water (approximate)
2 small cucumbers, like Kirby, or 1 English cucumber
1 cup snow peas
4 scallions
Handful of cilantro
2 chicken breasts, cooked and shredded (optional)

Cook the pasta.

In the bottom of the bowl in which you intend to serve the noodles, add the soy, rice vinegar, sesame oil, chili oil, salt and red pepper. Whisk in the peanut butter, and add enough water to get a thin, sauce-like consistency. (I find I usually need about ⅓ cup water.)

Peel the cucumbers and cut into thin matchsticks. Snap the ends off of the snow peas, and pull off any strings, then slice them. Thinly slice the scallions, and chop the cilantro.

When the pasta is cooked and drained, combine in the bowl with the sauce, using tongs to coat everything. Toss in the vegetables, the chicken if you are using it, give another toss, and serve.

NOTE: If you don't like the snow peas raw, you can toss them into the pasta water for the last minute that the pasta cooks, and then drain them with the pasta, to lightly blanch them.

Orzo with eggplant

Serves 8-10 as a side dish

This is great party food, particularly at things like barbecues. It keeps well and actually tastes better a day or two after you make it. This is the kind of dish you can make on the weekend and then nibble on all week long.

1 pound of orzo
1 large eggplant
2 red peppers
8–10 sun dried tomatoes, packed in oil
2 large tomatoes, chopped
2 cloves garlic, chopped
1 red onion, chopped
3-4 Tbsp balsamic vinegar
⅓ cup olive oil, plus oil for the eggplant
Handful of basil leaves, torn (optional)
Salt and pepper

Cook the orzo.

Place a few tablespoons of olive oil in a shallow dish. Slice the eggplant into rounds about ½ inch thick. Using a pastry brush, brush olive oil on both sides of each piece of eggplant, being careful not to use too much—the eggplant will soak up the oil very quickly. Season with salt and broil on each side until brown, about 4–5 minutes per side. Let the eggplant cool, then chop it up and put it in a large bowl.

Set the peppers under the broiler and cook, turning until they are black on all sides. Cool in a paper bag and then peel and chop the peppers and add to the bowl with the eggplant.

Continued . . .

Orzo with eggplant continued . . .

Chop up the sun dried tomatoes, and add them to the bowl, along with some of the oil they were packed in. Dice the tomatoes, chop the garlic, dice the red onion and throw it all into the bowl. Add the basil, if you are using it.

Toss the pasta into the bowl. Add the vinegar, olive oil, and salt and pepper to taste.

ON EGGPLANT: You can broil eggplant the way I described above, toss it with pasta, some of the pasta water, and some good Parmesan cheese and make a meal out of it. Or you can layer the broiled eggplant with store-bought marinara sauce and mozzarella cheese for a quick and easy eggplant parmigiana.

Pasta with sausage and mushrooms

Serves two

1 pint mushrooms
4 cloves garlic
Salt and pepper
½ pound sweet sausage
About one ounce of dried mixed wild mushrooms
½ cup white wine
1 small (14 oz) can plum tomatoes
Fresh thyme
½ pound pasta

Cook the pasta, reserving 1 cup of the pasta cooking water.

Put the wild mushrooms in a bowl and pour about ½ cup hot water over them. Let them soak.

Coarsely chop the mushrooms and set aside. Smash and chop the garlic, along with a pinch of salt, until it is a paste. Crumble the sausage into a hot pan and cook, stirring until the sausage browns. Add the mushrooms and the garlic, and cook until the mushrooms release their liquid. Remove the wild mushrooms from the liquid, squeezing them over the bowl, and chop. Add those to the pan, along with the liquid you soaked the mushrooms in. (Sometimes there is grit at the bottom of the mushroom liquid, so be careful not to add that. It won't, needless to say, enhance the dish….) Add the white wine, tomato, salt and pepper and fresh thyme, and simmer for 10–15 minutes. If the sauce gets dry, add some of the pasta cooking water.

Toss with cooked pasta and serve.

Pasta bolognese

Serves four, with an extra quart of sauce for the freezer

This is a staple in my house. This recipe will make enough sauce for a pound of pasta, with extra to stick in a quart container in the freezer, since it freezes so well. The only hitch is that if you have one pot, you have to make the sauce, then clear everything out of the pot to cook the pasta. I may be the laziest, most dirty-dish averse person on earth, but I still think it's worth the effort.

3 Tbs olive oil
1 large onion
2 medium carrots
3 celery stalks
3 cloves of garlic, minced
salt
red pepper flakes
1½ pounds ground beef
1 4 oz can tomato paste
1 cup red wine (whatever you have lying around)
1 14 oz can chicken stock (preferably low sodium)
1 28 oz can crushed tomatoes

Finely chop the onion, carrots and celery, and mince the garlic. Heat olive oil in a large pot over medium heat. Add the vegetables, a big pinch of salt, and red pepper flakes to taste, then sauté the vegetables until they are soft, about 10 minutes.

Add the beef, along with another pinch of salt, and brown the beef, breaking it up with a wooden spoon. It will take about 10 minutes to brown the beef. After it is brown, add the tomato paste and toast it until it slightly darker in color, about 5-8 minutes. Add the wine and stir, letting it reduce. Once the wine has reduced, after about 5 minutes, add the crushed tomatoes and the chicken stock. Stir everything together.

Bring the sauce to a boil and then reduce the heat to low. Let the sauce simmer until it thickens about 45 minutes. Taste and make sure there is enough salt – it might need more.

Freeze half of the sauce, and toss the rest with your favorite pasta. Don't forget to sprinkle the top with some good parmesan cheese!

Vegetables and Sides

VEGETABLES AND SIDES: You've got to eat them, so why not make them taste good? Sure, you can always just steam any given vegetable, or pop it into the microwave, but for very little additional effort you can actually enjoy getting your vitamins and minerals. So read on . . . .

Sesame bok choy

Serves two

I love bok choy this way. When it is sautéed quickly, the green leaves wilt but the white stems stay crisp, and it is absolutely delicious. Baby bok choy is best, but any size will do. Toasted sesame oil is not cheap, but it is well worth the investment. A little bit of this oil infuses any dish with a really nice, smoky flavor. It's especially nice with vegetables. Sometimes they sell sesame oil that contains canola oil, but bypass that for the real stuff. You can easily substitute snow peas for bok choy.

1 lb bok choy
Splash of peanut oil
Salt to taste
2 cloves garlic, chopped
2 tsp toasted sesame oil
1 Tbsp sesame seeds
Red pepper flakes, to taste

First, get the bok choy ready. If you are using baby bok choy, you can leave it whole, but with larger sizes of bok choy, simply cut off the ends and cut the leaves in half or thirds. It is better if some of the water from washing the vegetable is still clinging to the leaves.

Heat peanut oil in a large pan. When it is hot, throw in the bok choy and season with salt. Wait 2–3 minutes, until the green parts of the bok choy begin to wilt. (If the pan looks very dry, you can add a bit of water.) Add the garlic, give it a stir, and cook until the garlic just becomes fragrant, about 1 minute. Add the sesame oil and sesame seeds and serve.

Indian-style spinach and chick peas

Serve over rice

Indian food is one of those cuisines that I love to eat in restaurants but don't usually make at home. This recipe is the exception—it is very easy to make and can be a meal all by itself, with a little rice. Garam masala is a mixture of Indian spices that you can find in most grocery stores

1 lb baby spinach, coarsely chopped
1 can chickpeas
3 Tbsp olive oil
2 tsp cinnamon
1 medium onion, chopped
6 cloves garlic, chopped
1 inch piece of ginger, grated
4–6 plum tomatoes, chopped
2 tsp garam masala
1 tsp cumin
1 tsp salt

Heat oil over medium heat. Add the cinnamon and wait one minute. Then add the onions, season with salt, and cook until they are soft. Add the garlic and ginger and cook until fragrant, about 1 minute. Add the garam masala and the cumin, again cooking until fragrant, about 1–2 minutes. Add the tomatoes and cook until they start to break down, about five minutes. Add the chickpeas and cook until they start to soften, about 5–10 minutes. Then add the spinach and cook until the spinach is wilted. Taste and correct the seasoning.

Sautéed broccoli

Serves two

This is really just my version of stir-fry, and you can add any vegetables you want, but broccoli is my favorite, because it catches all that tasty sauce.

1 Tbsp peanut oil
1 Tbsp toasted sesame oil
Two cloves garlic, minced
½ tsp red pepper flakes
½ pound broccoli
2 Tbsp soy sauce
1 Tbsp rice wine
1 Tbsp rice vinegar
Splash of water (3–4 Tbsp)

Add the peanut oil, garlic and pepper flakes to a hot pan. When the garlic is sizzling and fragrant, but before it browns and burns, about one minute, add the broccoli. Give it a toss, and then add the soy sauce, rice wine, rice vinegar and a splash of water. Sauté until the broccoli is bright green and crisp-tender, add the sesame oil, and serve.

NOTE: You can add any number of vegetables to this dish, or even some chicken or shrimp to make a full meal.

Root vegetable slaw

You can use whatever root vegetables you like in this dish, or even go crazy and throw in some cabbage. The vegetables are all shredded together, which can be done with a box grater but takes all of 20 seconds if you are lucky enough to have a food processor with a grater attachment. The slaw can literally be assembled in less than 10 minutes, and it improves with age.

4 large radishes
½ small jicama
1 English cucumber (or 2 Kirby cucumbers)
1 small red onion
3 medium carrots
2 Tbsp soy sauce
Hot sauce to taste
2 Tbsp rice vinegar
2 tsp toasted sesame oil
1 inch of fresh ginger, peeled
4 scallions
Handful of cilantro

In the bottom of a large bowl, mix together the soy sauce, hot sauce, rice vinegar and sesame oil. Grate the radishes, jicama, cucumber, onion and carrot and add them to the bowl. Finely grate the ginger into the mixture. Slice the scallions, chop the cilantro and add both to the bowl. Mix well and serve.

Makes about four cups of slaw and tastes better a day or two later.

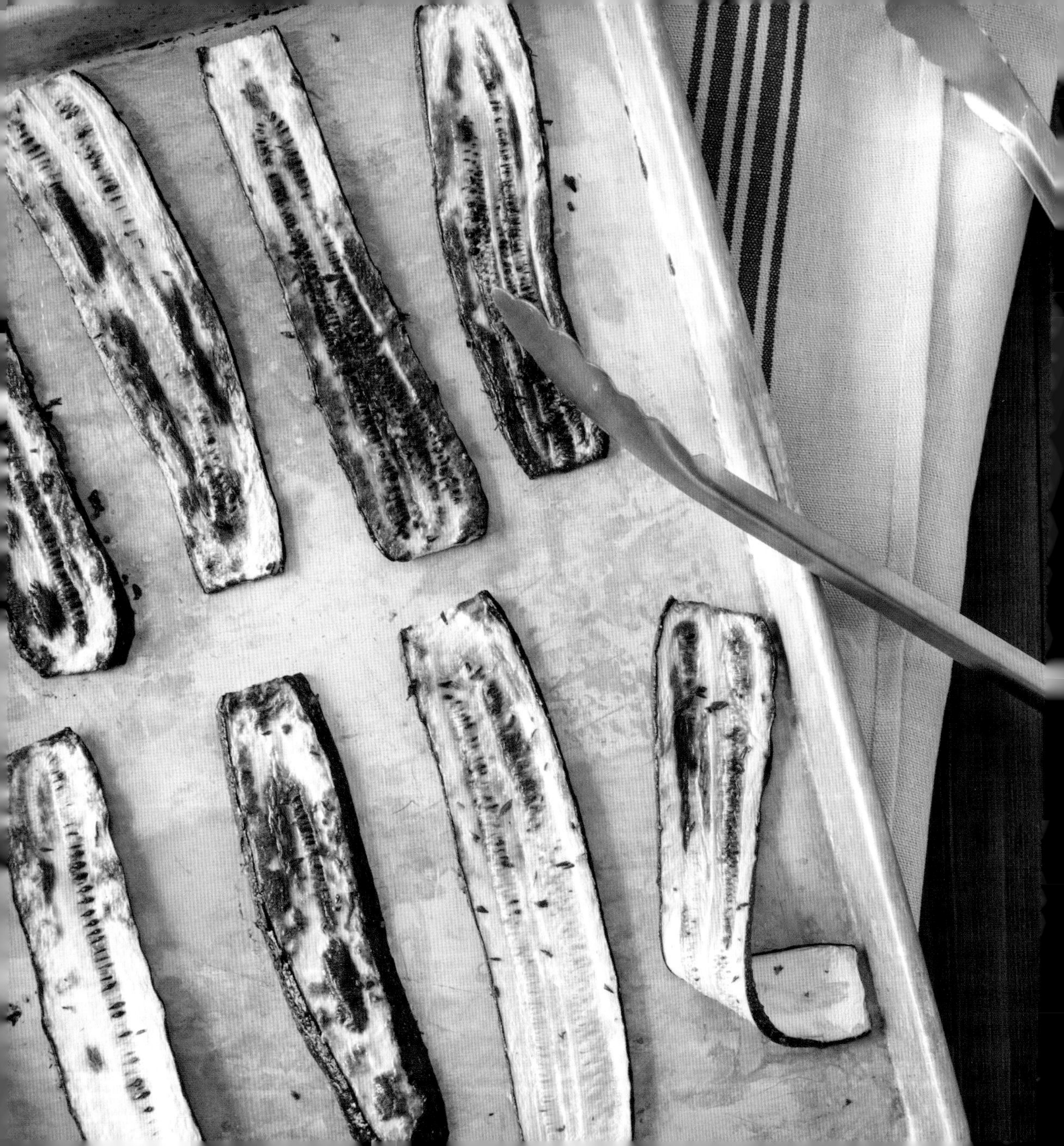

Broiled zucchini

Serves two

This is easy, absolutely delicious, and it takes only about 5 minutes to make.

3 medium zucchini
2 cloves garlic
Big pinch of salt
3 Tbsp olive oil
2 Tbsp fresh thyme

Slice each zucchini into long strips, about 1/4 inch thick. Smash the cloves of garlic with the side of a knife, sprinkle the garlic with salt, then chop the garlic and salt mixture into a paste.

Put the zucchini and garlic into a plastic bag along with olive oil. Finely chop the fresh thyme and add that to the bag. Seal it and shake the bag around until everything is well mixed.

Turn the broiler on, and cover a cookie sheet in aluminum foil. Lay the zucchini on the cookie sheet. Broil until each side is brown, about 3–5 minutes per side, depending on the broiler.

Serve hot or at temperature.

Spinach pie

Serves four

I really love spinach pie, and this is a terrific one. I used to be troubled by the Large Volume Spinach Problem: do I buy unwashed spinach, and spend an eternity ridding it of sand? Do I buy roughly a million packages of baby spinach to get the amount of cooked spinach I need? Do I just buy frozen spinach? Since I am lazy, I usually bought frozen spinach but was never quite happy with the results. Then one day I found the answer: organic frozen spinach. It really does make the best spinach pie. (If you don't believe me, conduct a blind taste test with your family and see what they say....)

One last comment: do not fear the phyllo dough! If you tear some of the phyllo sheets while assembling the pie, just keep going. It won't matter. If you don't want to use phyllo dough, buy frozen puff pastry dough and roll it out to a 12 inch rectangle.

- Two 10 oz packages of frozen spinach, defrosted and squeezed dry
- 8 sheets of phyllo dough
- 1 onion, chopped
- ¼ cup olive oil
- 2 eggs
- 3 scallions, thinly sliced
- ½ cup feta cheese
- ¼ cup pine nuts
- 5 Tbsp unsalted butter
- 4 Tbsp bread crumbs
- 3 Tbsp freshly grated Parmesan cheese
- 1 Tbsp sesame seeds
- Salt and red pepper flakes

Preheat oven to 375 degrees.

In a small dry pan, add the pine nuts and toast them, shaking the pan occasionally and watching the pan carefully, because nuts burn quickly.

In a large pan, heat the olive oil with the red pepper flakes. When the oil is hot, cook the onion until it is soft. Add the spinach, along with a generous pinch of salt, and cook until most of the liquid is gone. Cool the spinach slightly. Meanwhile, in a bowl beat the eggs with the feta cheese, pine nuts, 1 Tbsp of bread crumbs, and the sliced scallions. Mix in the spinach.

Continued . . .

Spinach pie continued . . .

Mix together the remainder of bread crumbs with the Parmesan cheese in a small bowl, and melt the butter in another small bowl.

Lay out a sheet of aluminum foil and on that lay the first sheet of phyllo dough. Brush it with butter, and sprinkle with the bread crumb-cheese mixture. Repeat with 7 more sheets of phyllo dough.

Pour the spinach mixture into the middle of the dough, then fold the phyllo dough up around the mixture. There should be a square of spinach in the center, not covered by phyllo dough. Brush butter on the top of the dough, and sprinkle the sesame seeds all over. Bake until it is golden, about 30 minutes. It is delicious warm or at room temperature.

Mashed cauliflower

Serves two, with leftovers

Cauliflower is easier to mash than potatoes, and with the addition of cheese it tastes almost as good. I like to use Gruyere cheese, but you can certainly use cheddar, or any other cheese that you like. Try it and see if you can fool your family into thinking they are eating potatoes....

1 head cauliflower, broken into small florets
¾ cup whole milk
2 Tbsp butter
1 tsp paprika
Salt and pepper
¾ cup of shredded cheese

Steam the cauliflower until it is soft, about 10 minutes. Transfer the cooked cauliflower to a pot and mash it until it has a relatively smooth consistency. Under low heat, stir in the milk, the butter and the paprika, and season with salt and pepper. Off the heat, stir in the cheese, and serve hot.

Roasted squash (and other vegetables)

Serves two

I'm almost embarrassed to include this recipe, because it is so easy, but it's a great trick and people love it. Literally, squash is cut into cubes, tossed with olive oil, salt and pepper, and roasted until brown. You can also spice it up with some cinnamon, cumin and chili powders.

If you like this dish, try roasting carrots or parsnips the same way.

For parties, I roast a whole mix of vegetables, including carrots, parsnips, zucchini, peppers, onions and eggplant, and it all tastes wonderful hot or at room temperature. Just increase the olive oil, salt and pepper to adequately coat the amount of vegetables you roast. Also, it is best to roast the vegetables in a single layer, so if you are roasting a lot of vegetables, use more than one cookie sheet.

1 large butternut squash
3 Tbsp olive oil
Salt and pepper to taste

Preheat the oven to 400 degrees. Peel the squash, scoop out the seeds, and cut into cubes. Toss the squash on a cookie sheet with olive oil, salt and pepper. Roast until the squash is golden on the outside, about 40–45 minutes.

Roasted potatoes

Serves two

For those of you who don't know how to roast potatoes, here it is. You can add any herbs and spices you want, and you can alter the flavors to match whatever else you're cooking. I like using Yukon Gold potatoes, which have a rich flavor and very thin skins, making peeling unnecessary. You can use whatever spices you like best. This is one recipe where I prefer garlic powder to fresh garlic, because it won't burn.

3 Tbsp olive oil
1½ tsp garlic powder
½ tsp cayenne pepper, or to taste
Generous pinches of salt and pepper
1½ pounds potatoes (peeled, if you prefer, and cut into wedges)

Preheat the oven to 400 degrees. On the tray where you plan to roast the potatoes, add the olive oil and spices. Toss the potatoes onto the tray and move everything around until it is well coated. Roast in the oven, shaking the tray occasionally and flipping the potatoes with a spatula once or twice, until the potatoes are brown and crisp, about an hour. Serve immediately.

ON POTATOES: The smaller you cut the potatoes, the faster they will cook. So if you're short on time, cut the potatoes into smaller pieces to cut down on the cooking time.

Fried rice

Serves two, with leftovers

Although the name implies otherwise, fried rice really doesn't have much fat, and it's a nice way to get some vegetables and some carbs with your protein. This dish is also great because you can basically dump in whatever vegetables you have on hand.

1 cup rice
1 Tbsp vegetable or peanut oil
1 tsp sesame oil
1 clove garlic, minced
½ cup onion, diced
½ cup carrot, diced
2 eggs
½ red pepper, diced
½ cup corn
2-3 Tbsp soy sauce
2 scallions, sliced

Cook the rice. Meanwhile, heat the vegetable oil in a large pan. Add the garlic, onion and carrot and sauté until the vegetables are soft. (If you are using any other root vegetable, add it at this time.)

Move the vegetables over to one side of the pan with a wooden spoon, and add the eggs. Scramble them with a fork or a wooden spoon until they are cooked. Add the red pepper and the corn and whatever other vegetables you have lying around. Stir everything together and sauté briefly.

When the rice is fluffy, add it to the pan, and toss it with the soy sauce and sesame oil, just until everything is coated. Sprinkle with scallions, stir, and serve.

Summer couscous

Serves two, with leftovers

Next time you're in the grocery store, please buy some couscous. It's easy to make and really versatile. Couscous is also great hot weather food because it cooks so quickly. This recipe is nice with Middle Eastern Spiced Chicken. Feel free to experiment with the vegetables; try some grated carrot, or even sweeten things up with a handful of raisins.

1 clove garlic, chopped
1 lemon
1 tsp cumin
Salt and pepper
3 Tbsp olive oil

1 cup couscous
2 scallions, thinly sliced
2 small cucumbers, diced
3 tomatoes, seeded and chopped, or one pint grape tomatoes, halved
½ red onion, diced
½ cup chickpeas (you can use canned, drained and rinsed)

Cook the couscous according to the instructions on the package.

In the bottom of a large, shallow bowl, whisk together the garlic, the juice of the lemon, cumin, salt, pepper and olive oil. Add all of the chopped vegetables and toss together. Mound the vegetables in the middle of the bowl, then spoon the couscous around the perimeter of the bowl.

Green beans with brown butter breadcrumbs

Serves two, with leftovers

This is also great with broccoli or asparagus, and you can really make this dish with any vegetable you want. It's barely even a recipe, but more of a way to jazz up vegetables. The brown butter is really tasty, and the panko–which are very crispy, Japanese style breadcrumbs that you can find in your grocery store–gives a nice crunch. Make sure to use fresh parmesan cheese, because it will make a big difference, flavor-wise.

1 pound green beans, with the strings pulled off and the ends trimmed
2 Tbs butter
2 Tbs breadcrumbs, preferably panko
1½ Tbs freshly grated parmesan cheese
Salt

Heat butter in a small pan over low heat. Cook the butter until it starts to turn golden, and smell nutty, about 10 minutes. Add the breadcrumbs, and toast them until they are also golden, another five minutes or so. Sprinkle the parmesan cheese into the breadcrumbs.

Steam the green beans in a pot with a little water in the bottom. When they are bright green, take them out, sprinkle them with salt, toss them with the breadcrumb mixture, and serve.

Foolproof Desserts

DESSERTS: I have a confession to make. I can't really bake. I hate to measure, and sifting is something that is just not in my vocabulary. So the recipes in this chapter are, trust me, idiot-proof. These are my stand-by desserts, for the occasions when I think a store-bought dessert just won't cut it. So all of you non-bakers out there, give these a try.

Fruit-topped cake

This is my mom's recipe, and it is the easiest, most versatile and tastiest dessert I know. If you are a baking novice, try this cake. It's really, really hard to screw up.

1 cup sugar
½ cup butter
1 cup flour (supposedly sifted, but I never do)
1 tsp baking powder
2 eggs
Pinch of salt

2-3 cups of the fruit of your choice, sliced (apples, pears, peaches and nectarines, or some combination, all work well)
1 lemon
Cinnamon
Sugar
¼ cup apricot preserves

Preheat the oven to 350 degrees. Cream the sugar together with the butter, beating until, well, creamy and pale (hence the name). Add the flour, baking powder and salt. Mix in the eggs, and then spread the cake in the bottom of a 9 inch springform pan.

After you slice the fruit, toss with the juice of one lemon to preserve the color. Place the sliced fruit in concentric circles on top of the cake. Sprinkle with cinnamon and sugar.

Bake at 350 degrees for one hour. After the cake has cooled, spread melted apricot preserves on top.

Rugulach

This was my great-grandmother's recipe. Rugulach are, concededly, a pain in the neck to make, but the result is worth the effort. They also freeze really well.

2 sticks butter
½ pound cream cheese
2 cups flour
1 tsp cinnamon
1 cup sugar
½ cup chopped walnuts
½ cup currants (you can use raisins, but I like currants because they're smaller)
Seedless raspberry or apricot jelly or ½ cup good quality chocolate chips

Preheat the oven to 375 degrees. Blend the butter, cream cheese and flour together. Divide the dough into four balls, flatten each ball, and refrigerate until chilled.

Mix together the cinnamon and sugar. Sprinkle a work surface with some of the cinnamon-sugar (much as you would flour a surface before rolling out dough). Roll out a ball of the dough, using the cinnamon-sugar as you would use flour, to prevent the dough from sticking, until it is about ¼ inch thick and a 12 inch circle. Spread a thin layer of jelly on top, then sprinkle with nuts and currants. In the alternative, simply sprinkle with nuts, currants and chocolate chips. Cut the circle into 12 wedges. Roll each wedge up, rolling from the outside toward the center, and place the cookies on a cookie sheet that has a Silpat on it. Sprinkle some cinnamon sugar over the top of the cookies.

Bake at 375 degrees for about 20 minutes.

NOTE ON BAKING: If you put too much jelly on the cookie, it will ooze out and burn all over the cookie sheet. This can be totally avoided by baking the cookies on a Silpat. If you don't have a Silpat and don't feel like shelling out the roughly $20 to buy one, you can also line the cookie sheet with parchment paper. Otherwise, be prepared to sacrifice some of your cookies.

1 TBSP
1/4 TSP

Bread pudding

Serve warm

I like this recipe because nothing needs to be measured exactly and it always winds up tasting delicious. This is a basic bread pudding recipe, and you can easily add all kinds of different flavors, like chocolate, pumpkin, apple, pecan or anything else you can think of.

6 cups of stale bread, torn into pieces
3 eggs
½ cup (1 stick) butter
½ cup sugar
½ cup brown sugar
1½ cups whole milk
1½ cups heavy cream
2 tsp vanilla
1 tsp cinnamon
½ tsp nutmeg
½ cup raisins

Preheat the oven to 350 degrees. Beat together the butter and both kinds of sugar. Beat in the eggs, then stir in the milk, cream, vanilla, cinnamon and nutmeg. Add the bread and stir until it looks saturated. Pour into a greased lasagna pan or casserole dish big enough to hold the entire pudding. Bake for 1½ hours.

Silver palate brownies

½ pound good semi-sweet chocolate (like Ghirardelli)
¼ cup chocolate syrup
1 stick unsalted butter
1 tsp vanilla extract
2 eggs, lightly beaten
¾ cup sugar
¼ cup flour
Pinch salt

Melt the chocolate in a small saucepan. Stir in the syrup. Remove from the heat and beat in the butter until smooth. Stir in the vanilla and the eggs and mix well.

In a bowl, sift (ha!) together the sugar, flour and salt. Add the chocolate mixture and mix well. Pour into a buttered and floured 8 inch square pan and bake 30 minutes.

NOTE: These brownies are rich, so this recipe doesn't make very much—they're supposed to be cut very small. I always double the recipe and make myself sick by eating too many of them.

Fruit crumble

Serves four

You can serve this over any fruit that is in season. This is another dessert I rely on because no sifting is required, and all amounts are approximate—in other words, you really can't screw this one up. Literally all you need to do is mix together the topping, cut up some fruit, dump it in a dish with a lemon juice and sugar, cover with the topping, and bake. It's terrific with some vanilla ice cream.

2 lb apples, pears, berries, stone fruit or some combination
1 Tbsp lemon juice (you can also use orange juice)
1 tsp lemon zest (you can also use orange zest)
2 Tbsp sugar
1 Tbsp flour

Crumble topping:

¾ cup flour
½ cup oats
½ cup light brown sugar, packed
6 Tbsp butter, melted
1 Tbsp cinnamon
½ tsp nutmeg
Big pinch of salt

Preheat oven to 350 degrees. Mix all of the crumble ingredients until they are in clumps. Set aside.

Cut whatever fruit you are using into uniform pieces. Dump the fruit into a large bowl and zest the lemon over the top. Add the sugar, flour and lemon juice. Taste the fruit, and if it is very sour you might want to sprinkle a bit more sugar.

Pour the fruit mixture into a large casserole dish and spread the crumble mixture evenly over the top. Bake until the fruit is bubbling and the topping is crunchy, about 30–40 minutes.

Blueberry squares

Makes about 16 squares and is delicious with vanilla ice cream

1½ cups flour
1 stick + 2 Tbsp butter
¼ cup + 2 Tbsp brown sugar
1/3 cup oats
½ tsp cinnamon
Salt

1 pint blueberries (about 2 cups)
½ cup seedless raspberry jam
½ tsp grated orange rind
1 Tbsp fresh orange juice
1 Tbsp flour

Preheat oven to 350 degrees. Grease an 8 inch square baking pan.

Mix together the flour, ¼ cup of brown sugar and a pinch of salt. Melt the stick of butter (about 12 seconds in the microwave should melt the butter) and mix that in. Press 2/3 of the mixture into the bottom of the baking pan and bake until it is just browned, about 20 minutes.

Melt the rest of the butter and add it to the remaining flour mixture, along with the oats, cinnamon and the rest of the brown sugar. Set aside.

In a separate bowl, mix together the blueberries, orange rind, orange juice, flour, and raspberry jam. (If you put the raspberry jam in the microwave for 15 seconds or so, it makes it much easier to mix.)

When the crust is cooked, pour the blueberry mixture on top, and then crumble the oatmeal mixture on top of the berries. Bake until the berries are bubbling and the topping is golden, about 30 minutes.

Pound cake filled with berries

This is one of my sister's go-to desserts. It looks beautiful and tastes delicious; the sour cream keeps the cake really moist.

½ cup unsalted butter at room temperature, plus more to grease the pan
1¼ cups sugar
1 Tbsp grated lemon zest
3 eggs
1 tsp vanilla
2 cups flour (plus extra for the pan)
½ tsp baking soda
1 tsp baking powder
½ tsp salt
¾ cup sour cream
1½ cups fresh raspberries or blackberries, or a combination
A little powdered sugar (optional)

Preheat oven to 350 degrees. Butter and flour an 8.5×4.5×2.5 inch loaf pan.

Put the butter in the microwave for 10 seconds to soften it up, then mix it with the sugar until light and fluffy. (You can do this with an electric mixer or a wooden spoon.) Mix in half the lemon zest. Add the eggs and mix until light and fluffy, then add the vanilla.

In another bowl, mix the flour, baking soda, baking powder and salt. Add a little of this to the wet ingredients then add some of the sour cream and mix. Continue alternating adding dry ingredients and sour cream until both are fully mixed in with the wet ingredients.

Wash and dry the berries, then gently mix them with the remainder of the lemon zest. You can add more lemon zest to taste, especially if the berries are very sweet.

Spread about half the batter (or a little less) into the loaf pan, then add the berries on top, leaving a rim of batter surrounding the berries. You might not fit all the berries. Then add the remainder of the batter on top.

Bake about an hour, until a toothpick comes out clean.

Dust with powdered sugar if you want. It's great served with vanilla ice cream or fruit sorbet.

Cranberry pistachio cookies

Makes about 2 dozen cookies

This is a gem of a recipe from Gourmet magazine. It's the perfect dessert recipe, because the cookies look fancy, taste delicious, and they are really easy to make.

1½ cups flour
½ tsp cinnamon
¼ tsp salt
1½ sticks of unsalted butter, softened
⅓ cup sugar
1 tsp freshly grated orange rind
½ shelled pistachios, coarsely chopped (don't use the red ones)
½ dred cranberries
1 egg, beaten
¼ cup coarse sugar

If the butter is not soft, an easy way to do this is by zapping it in a microwave for just 10 or 12 seconds.

Using an electric mixer, beat together the sugar, orange rind and softened unsalted butter in a bowl until it is light and fluffy. Mix in the flour, cinnamon and salt. Stir in the cranberries and pistachios until they are just combined. Gather the dough together, then divide it into two equal pieces, and roll each piece into a log about 2 inches in diameter. Wrap each log in plastic wrap and chill until they are very firm, at least an hour.

Preheat oven to 350 degrees. Brush beaten egg along the sides of the logs, then roll each log of cookie dough in coarse sugar, until it is pretty evenly covered. Alternatively, you can sprinkle the coarse sugar around each log until it is covered.

Cut each log into ¼ inch thick slices, then place the slices on a cookie sheet and bake until they are gold around the edges, about 15-18 minutes.

About the Author

Hope Korenstein loves food so she learned how to cook. She is an attorney by day and an intrepid home cook by night. She lives in Brooklyn with her husband and two children.

Photo credit: Joseph Merlone

Jennifer Silverberg is a commercial and editorial photographer who specializes in food, lifestyle, and portrait photography. A native New Yorker, she now makes her home in the Midwest. A place where the food grows, people work hard to harvest it, and then have dinner parties to celebrate it—Jennifer is happiest when photographing these experiences and, of course, sharing in the festivities along the way. She lives in Missouri with her husband, Joe, and their cat, Claire. Jennifer's images have been featured in *The New York Times*, *The Wall Street Journal*, *Parade Magazine*, and *You Magazine UK*, amongst others.

Inspiration

How I Escape "The Dinner Rut"

There are a lot of disadvantages to having a small kitchen, but there is one big advantage: that small kitchen is usually in a big city, which is full of really great food, and not just at four-star restaurants. I am lucky enough to live and work in New York City, a place that is filled with taco trucks, falafel stands, noodle joints, dumpling shops, pizza places, and sandwiches from banh mi to tortas. When I fall into a dinner rut, and I'm in need of some inspiration, I invariably find something new and different to sample. That gets me thinking about how to incorporate some of those new flavors into the dinners I cook, often with great results.

I also try to break out of the dinner rut at the grocery store, or, ideally, the farmer's market. If I see weird vegetables in the produce aisle that I've never noticed before, I'll take the plunge and buy them. If I can't find someone at the market who knows about the aforementioned weird vegetables, I usually go online and get information at http://www.epicurious.com.

Above all, I love to try new things. For every new food that tastes like dirty socks, there is something so delicious and amazing that I want to eat it over and over again.

Conversion Charts

METRIC AND IMPERIAL CONVERSIONS

(These conversions are rounded for convenience)

Ingredient	Cups/Tablespoons/ Teaspoons	Ounces	Grams/Milliliters
Butter	1 cup+16 tablespoons= 2 sticks	8 ounces	230 grams
Cream cheese1 tablespoon	0.5 ounce	14.5 grams	
Cheese, shredded	1 cup	4 ounces	110 grams
Cornstarch	1 tablespoon	0.3 ounce	8 grams
Flour, all-purpose	1 cup/1 tablespoon	4.5 ounces/0.3 ounce	125 grams/8 grams
Flour, whole wheat	1 cup	4 ounces120 grams	Fruit, dried 1 cup 4 ounces120 grams
Fruits or veggies, chopped	1 cup	5 to 7 ounces	145 to 200 grams
Fruits or veggies, pureed	1 cup	8.5 ounces	245 grams
Honey, maple syrup, or corn syrup	1 tablespoon	.75 ounce	20 grams
Liquids: cream, milk, water, or juice1 cup	8 ǻuid ounces	240 ml	Oats1 cup5.5 ounces150 grams
Salt	1 teaspoon	0.2 ounces	6 grams
Spices: cinnamon, cloves, ginger, or nutmeg (ground)	1 teaspoon	0.2 ounce	5 ml
Sugar, brown, firmly packed	1 cup	7 ounces	200 grams
Sugar, white	1 cup/1 tablespoon	7 ounces/0.5 ounce	200 grams/12.5 grams
Vanilla extract	1 teaspoon	0.2 ounce	4 grams

OVEN TEMPERATURES

Fahrenheit	Celcius	Gas Mark
225°	110°	¼
250°	120°	1⁄22
75°	140°	1
300°	150°	2
325°	160°	3
350°	180°	4
375°	190°	5
400°	200°	6
425°	220°	7
450°	230°	8

Index

R

S

T

V

ALSO AVAILABLE

Petite Eats

Appetizers, Tasters, Miniature Desserts, and More

by Timothy W. Lawrence

Petite Eats will inspire any host or hostess to throw a tasting party. Just as wine and beer tasting grow in popularity in homes and apartments across the country, tasting parties are gaining status as the new craze. Why not? With bite-sized treats, guests get to sample more food, and hosts get to showcase their culinary prowess with a wider range of hors d'oeuvres, desserts, and even miniature drinks. From classy avocado shrimp cups to sizzling bacon-wrapped jalapeños, chicken wings with spicy maple sauce to coconut petite fours, home cook Timothy W. Lawrence shows how anyone can whip up an amazing spread of small treats for any gathering.

Whether it's game night, a bridal shower, or a spur-of-the-moment get-together, *Petite Eats* makes entertaining fun and easy.

$14.95 Paperback • ISBN 978-1-62087-400-4

ALSO AVAILABLE

Perfect Parties, Second Edition

Recipes and Tips from a New York Party Planner

by Linnea Johansson

Foreword by Marcus Samuelsson

Have you always wanted to throw a glamorous party, the kind you've heard about but only ever dreamt of attending? Now you can, with priceless tips and ideas from Linnea Johansson, one of New York City's premier party planners. Each colorful page of this festive guide is stylishly shot and packed with invaluable advice for your next get-together. Johansson covers everything, from invitations to decorations, hors d'oeuvres to desserts, guest lists to gift bags. This updated second edition includes a brand-spanking-new chapter all about the bar, including some of the trendiest new drinks and one-of-a-kind concoctions you won't find in any other book — from hot toddies to refreshing, boozy snow cones, there's a drink here for any time of the year.

Whether you're looking to throw the perfect birthday bash, New Year's Eve extravaganza, anniversary surprise party, or just a quiet dinner party with close friends, *Perfect Parties* offers everything you need to know!

$22.95 Hardcover • ISBN 978-1-61608-867-5

ALSO AVAILABLE

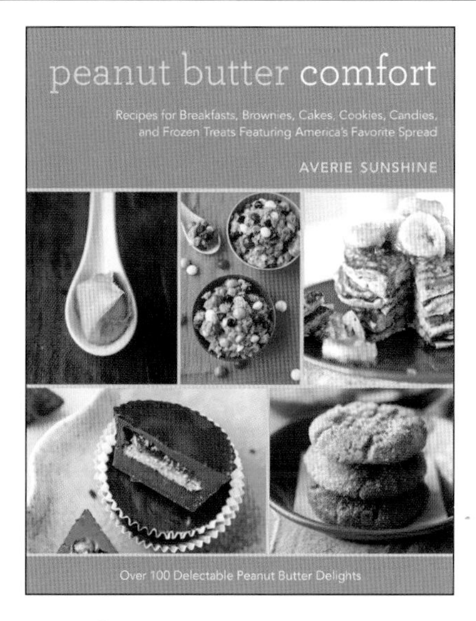

Peanut Butter Comfort

Recipes for Breakfasts, Brownies, Cakes, Cookies, Candies, and Frozen Treats Featuring America's Favorite Spread

by Averie Sunshine

Chock-full of decadent cakes, cookies, and candies, *Peanut Butter Comfort* is a delicious departure from your mother's PB&J. Here are recipes that showcase the rich, unmistakable flavor of peanut butter that we all love, as well as treats that highlight its subtlety and undeniable baking value. Averie Sunshine is a peanut butter aficionado; her easy-to-make recipes are imbued with her passion and creativity. Her vibrant, mouth-watering photographs bring each dish to life and will entice the casual snack-seeker and professional foodie alike.

Peanut Butter Comfort displays an astounding assortment of sweet, rich, decadent, soothing, and comforting treats. Any lover of peanut butter or quality comfort food will easily go nuts for this book!

$17.95 Hardcover • ISBN 978-1-62087-621-3

ALSO AVAILABLE

Dos Caminos Mexican Street Food

120 Authentic Recipes to Make at Home

by Ivy Stark with Joanna Pruess

After twenty years of traveling throughout Mexico, Chef Ivy Stark became enchanted by the colorful, tasty native foods and was determined to bring them to America. From stylish couples enjoying beef tacos at a café to day laborers standing at a counter over a paper plate filled with carnitas, everyone loves this delicious, accessible cuisine.

While the bright, robust flavors of Mexican cooking have tempted taste buds north of the border for decades, only recently has the country's lesser-known street food filtered onto the American table via California and the Southwest. Versatile and simple, these dishes can be enjoyed as a quick nibble or as part of an elegant meal. Stark introduces both beginners and skilled cooks to such traditional foods as Mexico City corn, smoked fish tostadas, plantain croquettes, and much more. Stark offers time-saving techniques and make-ahead suggestions, as well as tips for working with Mexican seasonings and produce like chilies and plantains.

$24.95 Hardcover • ISBN 978-1-61608-279-6

ALSO AVAILABLE

Cast Iron Cookbook

by Joanna Pruess

Photography by Battman

Cast iron is a unique material that heats evenly and lasts practically forever. Finally, here is a cast iron cookbook as timeless and varied as the material itself. Cast iron revolutionized American cooking upon its introduction, and soon no kitchen was complete without long-lasting, heat-retaining cast iron cookware. Today, cast iron is a fixture still, even the most cutting-edge, high-tech kitchens. Top chefs know: there is simply no other material quite like it. Classic illustrations of collectible pans and recipes for these or any cast iron products, combined with fresh takes on the best of American cooking, make the one-of–a-kind *Cast Iron Cookbook* an instant classic.

The recipes featured in *Cast Iron Cookbook* are tailored to the material's singular strengths, blending classic dishes like peach cobbler and fried chicken with modern fare like Duck with Apples, Moroccan Lamb-Stuffed Peppers, and Panko-Macadamia-Crusted Salmon.

$15.95 Paperback • ISBN 978-1-62087-260-4